# THE BIBLE EXPLORER'S GUIDE

## 1,000
### AMAZING FACTS AND PHOTOS

## PEOPLE AND PLACES

ZONDERkidz

ZONDERKIDZ

*The Bible Explorer's Guide People and Places*
Copyright © 2019 by Zondervan

This title is also available as a Zondervan ebook.

Requests for information should be addressed to:

Zonderkidz, 3900 *Sparks Dr. SE, Grand Rapids, Michigan 49546*

ISBN 978-0-310-76547-9

Published in association with the Books & Such Literary Management, 52 Mission Circle, Suite 122, PMB 170, Santa Rosa, California 95409-5370, www.booksandsuch.com

Zonderkidz is a trademark of Zondervan.

*Written by: Kathleen Bostrom*
*Art direction: Ron Huizinga*
*Design & layout: Michelle Lenger*

*Printed in China*

19 20 21 22 23 24 /DSC/ 22 21 20 19 18 17 16 15 14 13 12 11 10 9 8 7 6 5 4 3 2 1

# THE AMAZING CONTENTS

◄ p.7

p.31 ▼

▲ p.38

▲ p.62

◄ p.77

# THE ANCIENT WORLD

At the beginning of the book of Genesis, God creates the heavens and earth, land and sky, water, plants and animals, and humans.

▼ *Human life in the Bible begins in the Fertile Crescent. This is an area in the Middle East where much of human civilization and advancement flourished. Many believe this is where Adam and Eve lived in the garden, where Noah built his boat, and where God promised Abraham he would be the father of many nations.*

▼ *The people living in this region worshiped many gods. Often, each city-state had its own gods related to the sun, the moon, crops, fertility, and the weather.*

Black Sea

Caspian Sea

Mt. Ararat

Carchemish • ASSYRIA • Nineveh

Mediterranean Sea

Euphrates R.   Tigris R.

Jerusalem •

Babylon •

BABYLON

Arabian Desert

Persian Gulf

Red Sea

Possible sites for the Garden of Eden

| 0 | 300 km. |
| 0 | 300 miles |

▶ *The earliest writings and art from Ur are from the early Bronze Age (around 3000 BC).*

4

## THE TOWER OF BABEL

The Tower of Babel mentioned in the book of Genesis was built near an important city near modern-day Baghdad, Iraq.

## UR—ABRAHAM'S HOMELAND

Abraham was born, raised, and married in the city of Ur. This would have been located just across the river from the modern-day city of Nasiriyah, Iraq. Ur is one of the oldest cities ever discovered by archaeologists. It is estimated to be 6,500 years old.

▲ *This ziggurat is part of the remains of Ur. Scholars believe the Tower of Babel may have looked like this.*

# ADAM AND EVE

Adam and Eve are the first people mentioned in the Bible. God made heaven and earth. Then he created a beautiful garden and filled it with animals. God then formed Adam from dust and breathed life into him.

Knowing Adam would be lonely by himself, God put him into a deep sleep, took a rib from his side, and created Eve.

Adam and Eve lived in the beautiful garden. They had everything they needed. The only thing they didn't have was permission from God to eat from one very special tree—the Tree of the Knowledge of Good and Evil.

A serpent convinced Eve to eat the fruit from the forbidden tree. It was so tasty that she shared it with Adam. They broke God's one rule and that broke his heart. He sent them away from Eden forever.

Even then, God loved and cared for Adam and Eve. He even made clothes for them out of animal skins to protect them from the world beyond the Garden of Eden.

◀ *Eve was formed from one of Adam's ribs.*

## KEY WORD(S)

Names in the Bible have special meanings. Adam, from the Hebrew word *adam*, means "man." The name is also a play on the Hebrew word *adamah*, which means "earth." *Eve* is a pun on the words "to live." *Eden* means "paradise." Did you know that Adam didn't name Eve until they were leaving the garden? Originally, he called her "woman" because she was made from man.

## Did You Know?

The Bible never says that the fruit Adam and Eve ate was an apple. Apples aren't native to that part of the world. In paintings, it is often shown as an apple, a pomegranate, or an apricot.

## GET A CLUE!

Why did God put Adam in the Garden of Eden?

– Read: Genesis 2:15 –

The LORD God put the man in the Garden of Eden. He put him there to farm its land and take care of it.

**99**

## ONE MORE THING

The term "Adam's apple" refers to a harmless lump in the neck formed from the angle of protective cartilage around the voice box. It looks as though a person has a piece of apple caught in their throat. Men are more prone to an Adam's apple than women.

7

# CAIN AND ABEL (AND THE OTHER BROTHER)

After leaving Eden, Adam and Eve started a family. The firstborn, Cain, farmed the land while Abel, the second son, managed the family sheep.

One day, the sons made an offering to God. Cain brought the Lord fruit and Abel brought a sheep. God approved of Abel's gift, but not Cain's. This made Cain angry. God warned him to be careful and not let his anger get the best of him. Cain heard God's warning, but ignored him. He lured Abel out to a field, and in jealousy and anger, killed his brother.

God did not kill Cain, but sent him away from the only home he'd ever known. To protect Cain in the wilderness, God "put a mark" on him. He wandered until he ended up in the land of Nod, east of Eden.

Later, Adam and Eve had another son, Seth. He is described as being the "image" or "likeness" of his father. Seth became the son through whom the family line is traced all the way to Noah.

**KEY WORD(S)**
Nod, where Cain first lived after his banishment from home, comes from the Hebrew word for "restless," or "wandering."

## GET A CLUE!

What did Cain say to God when God asked him where his brother was?

– Read: Genesis 4:9 –

"I don't know," Cain replied. "Am I supposed to take care of my brother?"

**"**

## Did You Know?

Scholars debate what the "mark of Cain" might have been. An actual marking, like a tattoo? A defect that caused people to shy away from him? A skin disease, such as leprosy or boils? A horn? The 2nd century Jewish scholar, Abba Arikha (175–245 AD) even suggested that the mark referred to a dog that God gave Cain to protect him.

## ONE MORE THING

According to the book of Genesis, Cain's first son was named Enoch. Cain built a city and named it after his firstborn son. We cannot be sure where it was located.

*◄ If Cain did have a dog companion, it may have been a Canaan dog, which have lived in the Middle East for thousands of years.*

# NOAH

Noah was a descendant of Seth, the third son of Adam and Eve. Noah had a wife and three sons. He followed the ways of God when most people had become evil.

God was sad about what his beloved people were doing. He decided to wipe the earth clean and start over. But God saw the goodness of Noah, who "walked faithfully with God." (Genesis 6:9) God chose Noah to build an ark. He gave him specific instructions on how to build it. God then told him to gather a male and female pair of all the creatures on earth and put them on the ark along with all the food they would need.

After Noah and his crew were safely aboard, rain fell for 40 days and 40 nights, flooding the earth. It took close to a year before the waters went down enough for the ark to settle on dry land again. Then God placed a rainbow in the sky. It was a sign of his promise never to destroy the earth like that again.

## KEY WORD(S)
Noah's name is a play on words and means "relief," "comfort," and "rest." He may have had a lot of practice comforting his family and the creatures on the ark, but it's doubtful that he got much rest!

## GET A CLUE!
How did Noah know that the waters were going down and land would soon appear?

– Read: Genesis 8:11 –

"In the evening the dove returned to him. There in its beak was a freshly picked olive leaf! So Noah knew that the water on the earth had gone down."

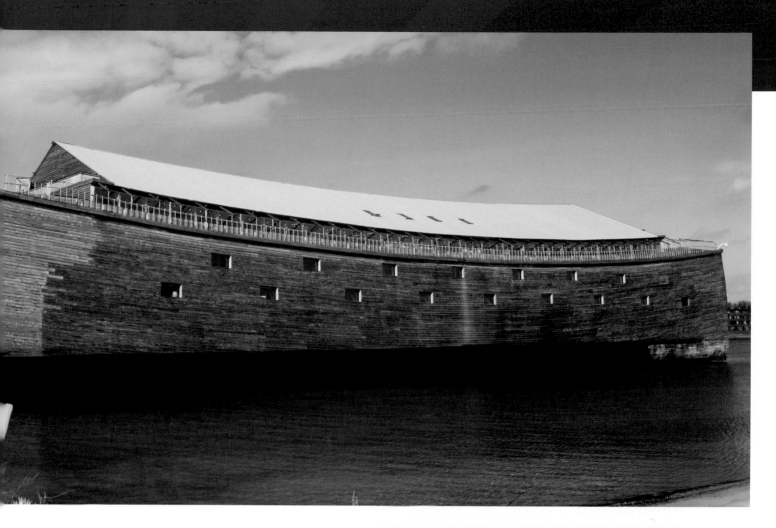

## ONE MORE THING

There are flood stories in other Middle Eastern traditions. One of the oldest was written on the flood tablet of the Babylonian Gilgamesh Epic.

▼ *Part of the Epic of Gilgamesh, a Babylonian flood story.*

### Did You Know?

A rainbow is actually a full circle. The lower half is hidden by land.

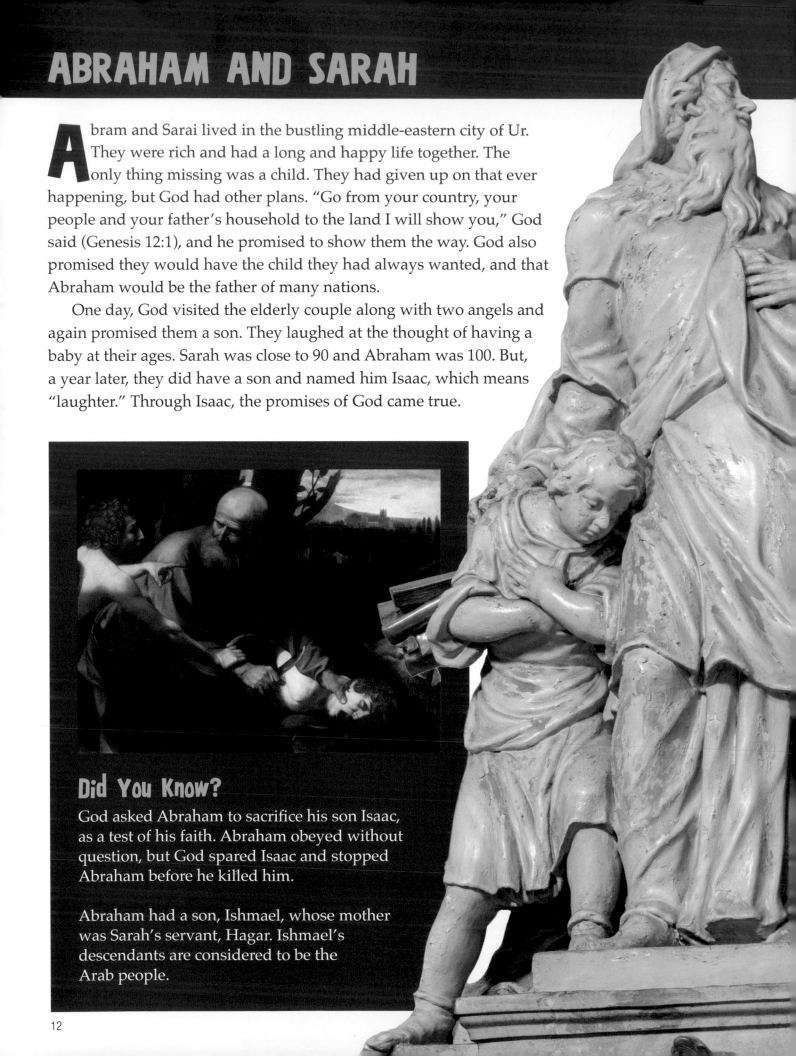

# ABRAHAM AND SARAH

**A**bram and Sarai lived in the bustling middle-eastern city of Ur. They were rich and had a long and happy life together. The only thing missing was a child. They had given up on that ever happening, but God had other plans. "Go from your country, your people and your father's household to the land I will show you," God said (Genesis 12:1), and he promised to show them the way. God also promised they would have the child they had always wanted, and that Abraham would be the father of many nations.

One day, God visited the elderly couple along with two angels and again promised them a son. They laughed at the thought of having a baby at their ages. Sarah was close to 90 and Abraham was 100. But, a year later, they did have a son and named him Isaac, which means "laughter." Through Isaac, the promises of God came true.

## Did You Know?

God asked Abraham to sacrifice his son Isaac, as a test of his faith. Abraham obeyed without question, but God spared Isaac and stopped Abraham before he killed him.

Abraham had a son, Ishmael, whose mother was Sarah's servant, Hagar. Ishmael's descendants are considered to be the Arab people.

## GET A CLUE!

What did Jesus say about Abraham?

– Read: John 8:56 –

Your father Abraham was filled with joy at the thought of seeing my day. He saw it and was glad.

► *Abraham's descendants lived in the land of Canaan.*

▼ *Abraham and his family traveled from Ur to Canaan.*

## KEY WORD(S)

God changed Abram and Sarai's names to Abraham ("father of multitudes") and Sarah ("princess") before Isaac was born.

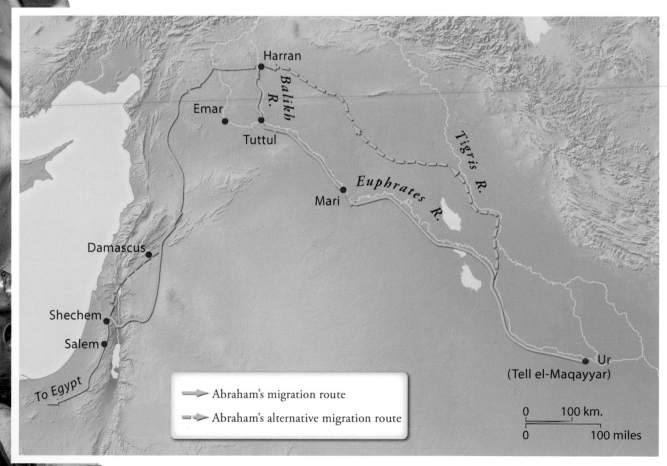

Abraham's migration route

Abraham's alternative migration route

0    100 km.

0    100 miles

# JACOB AND ESAU

Isaac, the son of Abraham and Sarah, married Rebekah, who gave birth to twin sons—Esau and Jacob. From early on, Isaac favored Esau and Rebekah favored Jacob. Esau became a skilled hunter, while Jacob preferred to stay close to home.

As the firstborn, Esau should have inherited all of Isaac's property. But Jacob tricked Esau into giving up his birthright. Then, Rebekah helped Jacob trick Isaac into giving the firstborn's blessing to Jacob. Esau vowed to get revenge on Jacob.

The two brothers grew up, married, and had families. After many years, Jacob sent word to Esau that he wanted to reunite. Esau met him partway and forgave Jacob, much to Jacob's surprise and delight.

Jacob's twelve sons become the Twelve Tribes of Israel.

▲ *Jacob receiving the firstborn blessing from Isaac.*

## GET A CLUE!

Esau traded his birthright to Jacob for a meal. What was the meal?

– Read: Genesis 25:34 –

Then Jacob gave Esau some bread and some lentil stew.

▶ *Lentils are part of the legume family, and just like beans and peas, lentils grow in pods.*

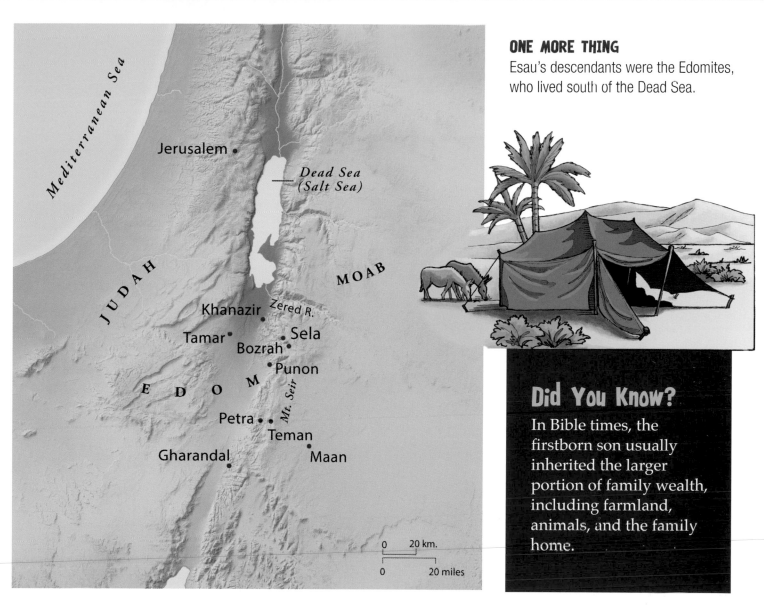

## ONE MORE THING
Esau's descendants were the Edomites, who lived south of the Dead Sea.

## Did You Know?
In Bible times, the firstborn son usually inherited the larger portion of family wealth, including farmland, animals, and the family home.

## KEY WORD(S)
The Bible says that Jacob and Esau were restless even in the womb. As Esau came into the world, Jacob grabbed his heel. The name *Jacob* means "heel" or "one who replaces."

► *Another Biblical set of twins is found in Genesis 38. Their names were Perez and Zerhah.*

# EGYPT

For a long time, Egypt was considered two completely different lands. The water lily was the symbol for the Upper region and the papyrus plant symbolized the Lower region. The Israelites of Joseph's time settled in Lower Egypt.

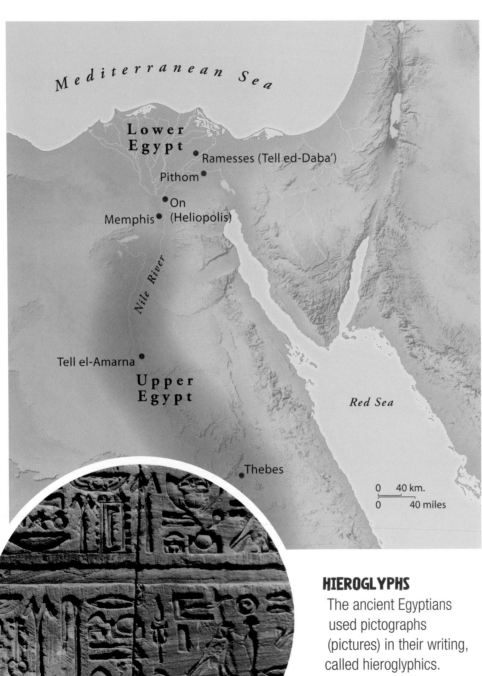

Mediterranean Sea

**Lower Egypt**

Ramesses (Tell ed-Daba')

Pithom

On
Memphis (Heliopolis)

Nile River

Tell el-Amarna

**Upper Egypt**

Red Sea

Thebes

0    40 km.
0       40 miles

### HIEROGLYPHS
The ancient Egyptians used pictographs (pictures) in their writing, called hieroglyphics. Once experts understood what the hieroglyphs meant, they were able to read many of the carvings found in tombs and temples throughout Egypt.

### BURIED TREASURE
Ancient Egyptians built many tombs to bury pharaohs and other people of high rank. Buried with these people were gold-covered death masks, ancient musical instruments, food, servants, and other treasures.

## RUINS

The ancient Egyptians prized their monuments. Temples and tombs make up most of the ruins that have been found buried beneath Egypt's sand.

▲ *The Pyramid of Djoser is an example of a step pyramid and is thought to have been built in the 27th century BC.*

▲ *The most well-known pyramids in Egypt are the three found in Giza. These pyramids had already been standing for about 1,000 years when Abraham first went to Egypt.*

## THE NILE RIVER

The only river in Egypt is also the longest river in the world. The Nile floods every year, giving the land around it fresh, fertile soil for certain periods of time. In the book of Exodus, the Nile River is the river where baby Moses was placed by his mother, in hopes that someone would rescue him, saving his life from the pharaoh who wanted to kill all the Israelite baby boys at the time.

# JOSEPH (AND HIS BROTHERS)

Joseph was the eleventh of Jacob's twelve sons. He was the firstborn of Rachel, Jacob's favorite wife. According to the Bible, Joseph's father loved him more than his other sons, which caused many of his brothers to hate him. The brothers set out to kill him. Reuben, the oldest, convinced the others to spare Joseph's life. They stripped him and threw him into an empty well. Later they sold him for twenty pieces of silver to a caravan of merchants on their way to Egypt.

After some struggles in Egypt, Joseph became a trusted official in charge of storing food for all of Egypt. When a famine came, the Egyptians did well. Back in Canaan, however, Joseph's family ran out of food. They traveled to Egypt to ask for food. Joseph knew them immediately, but they did not recognize him. Once his brothers proved themselves worthy, Joseph told them who he was. He forgave them and said that God had brought him to Egypt to save them. Pharaoh offered to give Joseph's family a safe place to live, and they brought everyone, including their father, Jacob, to settle in Egypt.

▶ *Joseph's father gave him a special robe. This kind of garment is ornamental and not suitable for working. It is sometimes referred to as the "coat of many colors." When Joseph's brothers sold him into slavery, they soaked his coat in goat's blood and told their father an animal had attacked Joseph.*

## GET A CLUE!

What did Jacob ask Joseph to promise him after his death?

– Read: Genesis 47:29b–30 –

Don't bury me in Egypt. When I join the members of my family who have already died, carry me out of Egypt. Bury me where they are buried. ❞

▼ *Tradition says Jacob is buried in the Tomb of the Patriarchs.*

## Did You Know?

Joseph had some special dreams. In one of them, he and his brothers are bundling up grain in the field. The brothers' bundles bow down to Joseph. In another dream, the sun, moon, and stars bow down to Joseph. This is why his brothers resented him. They assumed he thought he was better than they.

### KEY WORD(S)

After Joseph explained some of Pharaoh's dreams to him, Pharaoh renamed him *Zaphenath-paanea*. Many scholars have debated the meaning of this name from "revealer of secrets" to "preserver of the world" to "the god speaks [and] he lives."

The descendants of Joseph and his brothers lived in Egypt for four hundred years. The Hebrews grew in number, and were forced to be slaves by the Egyptians. To stop Hebrew population growth, it was announced that Pharaoh wanted all male babies killed.

At this time a Hebrew couple gave birth to their third child, a boy. To save him, his mother placed him in the Nile River in a basket. A princess rescued and adopted him, naming him Moses.

Even though Pharaoh's daughter raised Moses, he knew of his connection to the Hebrew people. God heard the people's cries for help and chose Moses to lead them out of slavery to freedom in the land that had once been theirs. Not wanting to lose his slaves, Pharaoh forbid them to leave Egypt. God sent ten terrible plagues, but nothing changed Pharaoh's mind. That is, until the last one, which resulted in the deaths of all the firstborn sons of Egypt, including Pharaoh's own son. Pharaoh let the Hebrew people go, but after they fled, he changed his mind. He sent his armies after them. God parted the Red Sea so the Israelites could walk across it, but Pharaoh's soldiers drowned as they followed.

It took forty years for Moses and the people to reach the promised land, Canaan. Moses died just before they arrived, but God allowed him see it from a mountaintop before his death.

*Mediterranean*

Baal Zaphon
Rameses (Pi-ramesse)
Pithom • / • Succot
*Wadi Tumilat*
*Bitter Lakes*
*Nile River*
*Red Sea*

0   40 km.
0   40 miles

## Did You Know?

Moses was the only person allowed to see God's face. This happened when God met with him on the top of Mt. Sinai to give him the Ten Commandments. The commandments were laws for the people as they traveled in the desert and for his people even to now.

Probable route of the Exodus
Alternative route

Sea

Lake Balah
Lake Timsah

Sinai
Peninsula

Mt. Sinai

## KEY WORD(S)

*Exodus* comes from a Greek word that means, "exit" or "the way out." The story of Moses and the journey from Egypt is found in Exodus, the second book of the Bible.

## ONE MORE THING

God guided the people across the desert in a cloud during the day and a column of fire at night. And God appeared to Moses as a burning bush. An appearance of God is called a theophany.

▼ *Some traditions say that Joseph is buried near ancient Shechem.*

## GET A CLUE!

What did Moses make sure to take with him when the people left Egypt?

– Read: Exodus 13:19 –

Moses took the bones of Joseph along with him. Joseph had made the Israelites give their word to do this. He had said, "God will surely come to help you. When he does, you must carry my bones up from this place with you."

# AARON AND MIRIAM

**M**oses had a sister and a brother—Miriam and Aaron. Although Moses was the leader of the exodus to free the Israelites from Egypt, Miriam and Aaron also had important roles in the story.

After Moses's birth, when his mother hid him in a basket in the Nile river, Miriam convinced the princess to (unknowingly) hire their mother to nurse the baby.

Moses wasn't sure about leading the people because he had a speech impediment. God appointed Aaron to be Moses's spokesperson. For the most part, the two brothers worked as a team.

Later, Aaron became Israel's first high priest, in charge of organizing and presenting offerings to God. Aaron's sons in turn became priests, as did the tribe to which the family belonged, the Levites.

Both Aaron and Miriam made mistakes. They opposed Moses because of his marriage to a foreign woman. This made God angry, and Miriam, for a time, was stricken with leprosy. When the Israelites lost faith that Moses would return from a talk with God, Aaron built a golden calf for them to worship.

## KEY WORD(S)

Every year, as an act of worship, Aaron would choose two goats. One goat became a sacrifice and the other, a *scapegoat*, was sent into the desert symbolically carrying the people's sins away. The term *scapegoat* is still used today to refer to someone who takes the blame for another person.

◄ *In 1990, archaeologists found a silver calf at Ashkelon. It provides important evidence to show how people in this area worshiped.*

## GET A CLUE!

What was the first miracle that God told Aaron to perform?

– Read: Exodus 7:9 –

Take your walking stick and throw it down in front of Pharaoh. It will turn into a snake. "

## ONE MORE THING

The bull is often used as a symbol of strength. In the time of the exodus, the bull was also associated with numerous pagan gods. The golden calf, made from the people's gold jewelry and belongings, was a sign that the people were turning away from God.

## Did You Know?

After Pharaoh's armies drowned in the Red Sea while chasing after the Israelites, Miriam, considered to be a prophetess, led the women in a song about the greatness of God. Some verses of Miriam's song are included in Psalm 107, and were originally meant to be sung.

# JOSHUA AND RAHAB

Joshua, son of Nun, served as a military leader under Moses. He was the only person allowed to go with Moses to the top of Mt. Sinai when God inscribed the stone tablets with the Ten Commandments. Joshua stayed in a tent and did not speak with God.

As the promised land drew near, God commanded Moses to name Joshua as his successor. When the time came to cross into the promised land, Joshua led the way.

Joshua sent two spies ahead of the rest of the army to Jericho, a great, walled city near the Jordan River. A woman named Rahab hid the spies, and then later helped them escape. Like others in Jericho, she had heard stories of how the Israelites had escaped Egypt. Rahab chose to believe in their God. She asked the spies to spare her and her family when they returned to attack the city of Jericho.

God told Joshua to march the armies around the city for six days. On the seventh day, at Joshua's command, the priests blew seven trumpets. The Israelites let out a great shout, and the walls around Jericho collapsed. They killed everyone in Jericho, except for Rahab and her family.

Before Joshua died, he divided up the land to all the tribes of Israel, as had been promised to them by God since the time of Abraham.

## KEY WORD(S)

Moses changed the name of *Hoshea*, which means "salvation," to *Joshua* (Yehoshu'a), a name that means "the Lord saves," or "the Lord gives victory." Interestingly, the name *Jesus* (Yeshu'a) also has the same root as *Joshua*, but with Greek and Aramaic influences.

## ONE MORE THING

The horns (shofar) used by the Israelites in Jericho were made of ram's horns. Like modern trumpets, a person's lips, teeth, tongue, and facial muscles controlled the varying sounds and pitch.

▲ *Artist depiction of Jericho at the time of conquest.*

## Did You Know?

Rahab married an Israelite, Salmon, and they had a son, Boaz. Her great-great-great grandson, David, would one day become a mighty king in Israel. Jesus would be born into the family tree of David.

## GET A CLUE!

How did the Israelite army know where to find Rahab and her family when they came to destroy Jericho?

– Read: Joshua 2:17–18 –

The spies had said to her, "You made us give our word. But we won't keep our promise unless you do what we say. When we enter the land, you must tie this bright red rope in the window. Tie it in the window you let us down through."

,,

# ISRAEL

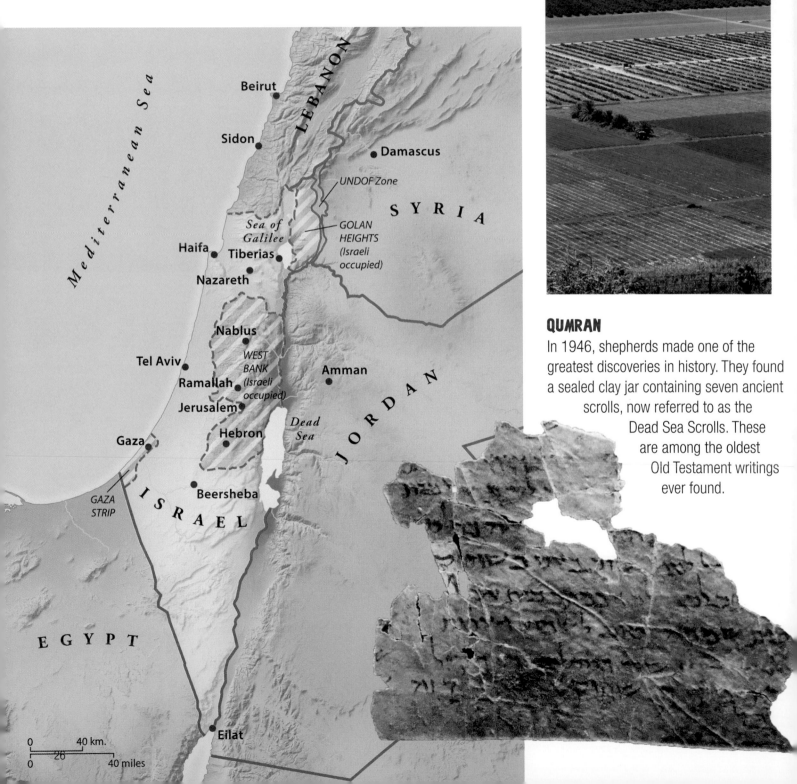

**M**odern-day Israel encompasses some of the land that was promised to Abraham and his descendants. It is part of the land of Canaan that Joshua portioned out to the twelve tribes of Israel. Before the Israelites migrated to Canaan, they were promised a land flowing with milk and honey. To this day, Israel grows diverse crops, despite sometimes harsh growing conditions.

Mediterranean Sea

Beirut

Sidon

LEBANON

Damascus

UNDOF Zone

Sea of Galilee

GOLAN HEIGHTS (Israeli occupied)

SYRIA

Haifa

Tiberias

Nazareth

Nablus

WEST BANK (Israeli occupied)

Tel Aviv

Ramallah

Amman

Jerusalem

Dead Sea

JORDAN

Gaza

Hebron

GAZA STRIP

ISRAEL

Beersheba

EGYPT

0       40 km.
0       40 miles

Eilat

## QUMRAN

In 1946, shepherds made one of the greatest discoveries in history. They found a sealed clay jar containing seven ancient scrolls, now referred to as the Dead Sea Scrolls. These are among the oldest Old Testament writings ever found.

## WATER WORLD

At the southern end of Israel, in the Gulf of Eilat, divers can see many marine fish, beautiful coral, and some interesting ship-wrecks as they explore.

◄ *More than half of Israel's population lives on the coastal plain, a strip of land along the Mediterranean Sea.*

► *The Dead Sea is the lowest and saltiest point on earth. The water is so salty that you can float effortlessly.*

## BETHLEHEM

The settlement of Bethlehem dates back to at least 1400 BC where it is mentioned in a letter to Pharaoh from an Egyptian governor of Jerusalem. It is known as the hometown of both King David and Jesus and was the home that Ruth and Naomi returned to from Moab.

# DEBORAH AND GIDEON

Following the deaths of Joshua and the elders who came after him, the people of Israel found themselves without an obvious leader. Although they settled in the long-awaited promised land, they abandoned God's laws and did as they pleased. To get the people back on track and return them to their faith, God raised up new leaders, known as judges.

Two of the judges were Deborah and Gideon. Deborah, a descendant of Joseph, is the only female judge named in the Bible. God appointed her when the Israelites cried for help after suffering twenty years of oppression under the cruel Canaanite king, Jabin. Deborah, Barak, and Jael worked together to defeat Jabin and Sisera, his military commander.

Peace reigned for forty years until the Israelites once again turned away from God. Invaders were destroying their land. God sent an angel to a man named Gideon, asking him to be the Israelites' next leader. Gideon gathered an army to attack the Midianites. One night, the Israelite army surprised the enemy camp by shining bright torches and blowing trumpets. This caused so much confusion that the Midianites ended up killing each other. Those who survived fled in terror, thus giving Gideon and his army the victory.

## Did You Know?

In the Bible, judges are not like modern judges who serve in courtrooms. Although her main responsibility was military in nature, Deborah often sat under a date palm tree and people came to her with their troubles.

When Gideon selected his army, God told him to choose only those men who drank from the river using their hand for a scoop instead of drinking directly from the river.

## KEY WORD(S)

After Gideon's victory, he gathered the gold of the defeated people. He made himself an *ephod*, an elaborate linen garment worn by the high priest then built an idol that his people began to worship, breaking the first commandment and turning from the ways of God, who had called him to service.

## GET A CLUE!

Where did the angel of the Lord first find Gideon and what was he doing which would be considered odd?

– Read: Judges 6:11 –

The angel of the LORD came. He sat down under an oak tree in Ophrah. The tree belonged to Joash. He was from the family line of Abiezer. Gideon was threshing wheat in a winepress at Ophrah. He was the son of Joash. Gideon was threshing in a winepress to hide the wheat from the Midianites.

"

## ONE MORE THING

The Song of Deborah (Judges 5:2–31) is unique from other songs in the Bible because it celebrates the military victory of two women, Deborah and Jael.

# SAMSON AND DELILAH

**B**efore Samson's birth, an angel told his parents that their son was chosen to be a lifelong servant of God. Samson was strong and powerful, but he did not always live a godly life. He was physically strong but weak in character. He demanded his own way and killed those who offended him. He insisted on marrying a Philistine woman, which was a great offense to the Israelites. (The Philistines were the longtime enemies of the Israelites.)

Samson met another Philistine woman named Delilah. The Philistines wanted to know what gave Samson his strength so they offered Delilah silver to discover his secret. Samson confessed to Delilah that his power came from his long hair, which had never been cut. One night while Samson slept, Delilah had his hair cut. The Philistines easily caught him, gouged out his eyes, threw him in prison, and made him a slave.

The Philistines planned a huge gathering that included all their rulers. Samson was called to the temple to put on a show. After a prayer to God, and with one last burst of strength, he pushed down the pillars holding up the structure and everyone died, including Samson.

## KEY WORD(S)

*The Philistines* were first known as *Peleshets*, a name used to refer to foreigners or wanderers. *Philistine* in Greek is *Palestine*. The word *philistine* has come to mean someone who is materialistic, preoccupied with gathering wealth and possessions.

▼ *The Philistines were known as great warriors and seafarers.*

## GET A CLUE!

What did Samson use to kill over 1,000 Philistines after his own people turned him in?

– Read: Judges 15:15 –

He found a fresh jawbone of a donkey. He grabbed it and struck down 1,000 men.

## Did You Know?

Before Samson's birth, an angel told his parents to raise him as a Nazirite, a person set aside to give his or her life in service to God. A Nazirite could not drink anything made of grapes, including alcohol and vinegar. Cutting one's hair was also banned, which is why Samson's hair gave him his strength—it represented his holy calling.

### ONE MORE THING

Each of the Philistine rulers paid Delilah about twenty-eight pounds of silver, an enormous fortune, for her betrayal of Samson.

# RUTH AND NAOMI

Ruth is one of only two women in the Bible with an entire book named after her. The other one is Esther.

Ruth lived in Moab on the eastern side of the Dead Sea. She married an Israelite, whose family had originally lived in Bethlehem. She lived with her husband and his parents, including his mother, Naomi. When Naomi's husband and sons died she told her daughters-in-law, Ruth and Orpah, that she wanted to return to her homeland. They were free to stay and remarry. Ruth chose to go with Naomi and to worship Naomi's God, the God of the Israelites. "Your people will be my people. Your God will be my God," she told Naomi. (Ruth 1:16)

Once in Bethlehem, Ruth worked in the fields of a man named Boaz. Ruth picked up the barley grain left on the ground after the completion of the harvest. Boaz was related to Naomi's husband. When he learned of this connection and how in need Ruth and Naomi were, he decided to protect them. Boaz and Ruth married and became the parents of Obed, who would become the great-grandfather of David, the future king of Israel.

## ONE MORE THING

Ruth is one of only four women listed in the gospel of Matthew's genealogy of Jesus.

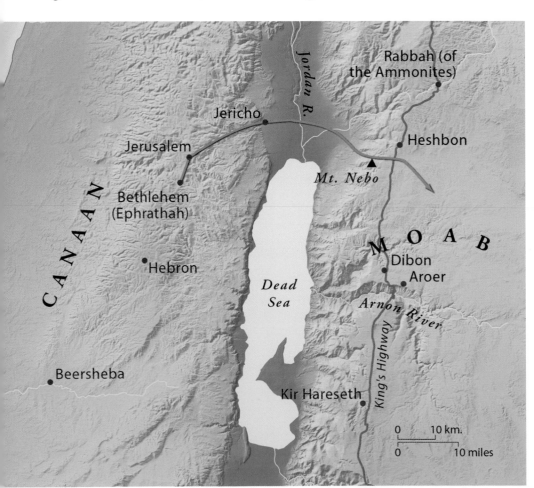

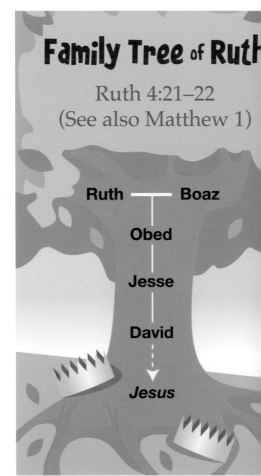

## Family Tree of Ruth

Ruth 4:21–22
(See also Matthew 1)

Ruth ——— Boaz

Obed

Jesse

David

*Jesus*

### KEY WORD(S)
*Bethlehem* means "house of bread," and was a prosperous land by the time Naomi returned with Ruth.

## GET A CLUE!
How was a business deal in Israel made legal in the time of Ruth and Naomi?

– Read: Ruth 4:7 –

In earlier times in Israel, there was a tradition or practice used when family land was bought back and changed owners. The practice made the sale final. One person would take his sandal off and give it to the other. That was how people in Israel showed that a business matter had been settled.

▲ *Aerial view of Bethlehem and fields nearby.*

◀ *This ancient sandal is from the 16th century BC and is made of leather.*

## Did You Know?
Scavenging the fields for grain was what people did to keep from starving when they had no source of income. Barley, perhaps the most important crop, was used to feed the livestock and make bread.

# HANNAH AND SAMUEL

A man named Elkanah had two wives, Hannah and Peninnah. Elkanah loved Hannah deeply, but they had no children together, whereas Peninnah had many children. Penninah made fun of Hannah because of this, which made Hannah very sad. Once a year, the family traveled to Shiloh to offer sacrifices to God. As Hannah prayed in the temple by herself, she broke down crying and prayed to God for a son, whom she promised to give to God for his service.

Hannah did become pregnant. When her son, Samuel, was born, she kept her promise. After the baby was weaned, she took him to the temple in Shiloh and gave him to the care of the priest, Eli.

Eli's two sons were not good men and they were cruel to Samuel. God chose Samuel to serve as Eli's assistant, rather than Eli's own children. After Eli died, the people of the land recognized Samuel as a prophet, and respected and honored him. He served God faithfully his entire life. After the people asked for a ruler, Samuel was the prophet who anointed Saul the first king of Israel.

## Did You Know?

After Samuel went to live in the temple with Eli and to serve him, Hannah prayed aloud a song of rejoicing. In this prayer-song, she praised the glory of God and predicted a future king. Because of this, Hannah is called a prophetess.

## KEY WORD(S)

Hannah named her firstborn son *Samuel*, meaning "heard by God," because he was the answer to her prayer in the temple. After he begins serving in the temple, Samuel is awakened by God's voice calling to him.

## GET A CLUE!

Who were the people really rejecting as a leader when they asked Samuel to appoint a king to take his place?

– Read: 1 Samuel 8:7 –

The LORD told him, "Listen to everything the people are saying to you. You are not the one they have turned their backs on. I am the one they do not want as their king."

**ONE MORE THING**

In biblical times, it was very important that a family have children to carry on the line through the father. A woman's job was to have children for her husband. This is why Hannah was so sad.

# KING SAUL

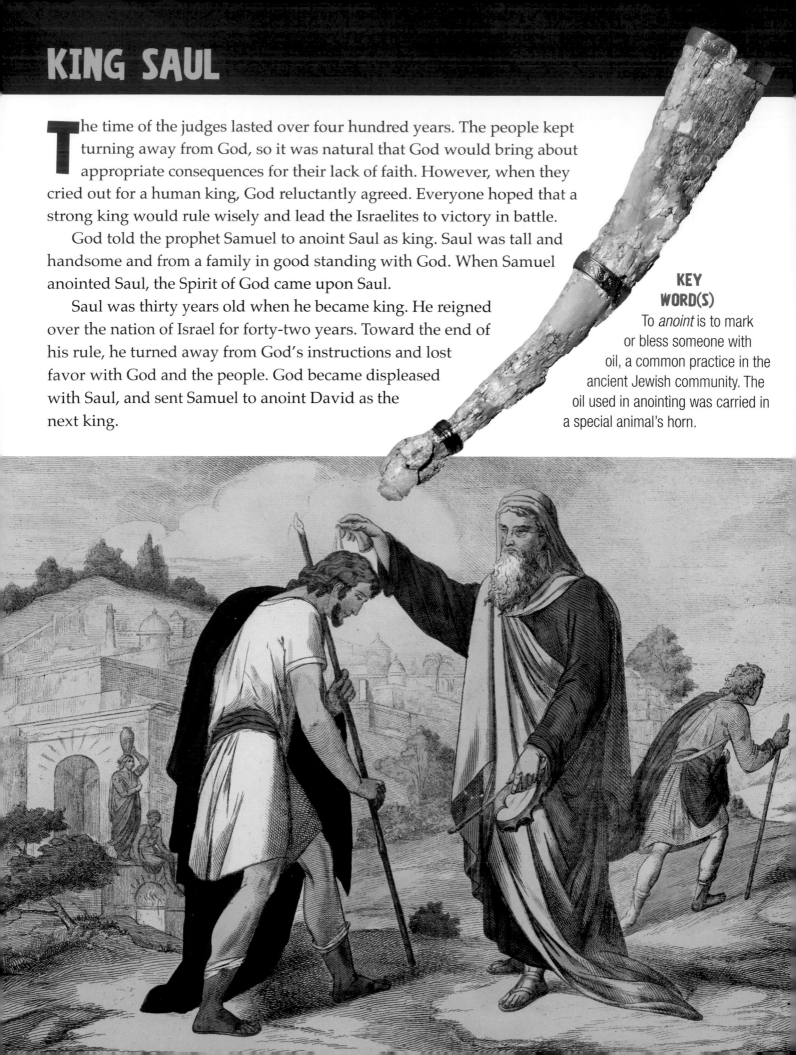

The time of the judges lasted over four hundred years. The people kept turning away from God, so it was natural that God would bring about appropriate consequences for their lack of faith. However, when they cried out for a human king, God reluctantly agreed. Everyone hoped that a strong king would rule wisely and lead the Israelites to victory in battle.

God told the prophet Samuel to anoint Saul as king. Saul was tall and handsome and from a family in good standing with God. When Samuel anointed Saul, the Spirit of God came upon Saul.

Saul was thirty years old when he became king. He reigned over the nation of Israel for forty-two years. Toward the end of his rule, he turned away from God's instructions and lost favor with God and the people. God became displeased with Saul, and sent Samuel to anoint David as the next king.

### KEY WORD(S)
To *anoint* is to mark or bless someone with oil, a common practice in the ancient Jewish community. The oil used in anointing was carried in a special animal's horn.

## Did You Know?

Before he was king, Saul raised donkeys for his father. He was a shy man who is described as: "as handsome a young man as could be found anywhere in Israel, and he was a head taller than anyone else." (1 Samuel 9:2)

## ONE MORE THING

Saul lost favor with God and God would no longer talk to him. He secretly went to a medium to find out what he should do, even though he himself had said that was illegal. In a strange twist, the image of Samuel, who was dead, appeared to the medium and predicted that the Israelites would be defeated by the Philistines and Saul and his sons would die.

Saul is wounded in a battle with the Philistines. Rather than be killed by his enemies, he throws himself on his own sword.

### GET A CLUE!

What was the name of Saul's son who became David's best friend?

– Read: 1 Samuel 20:42 –

Jonathan said to David, "Go in peace. In the name of the LORD we've promised to be friends. We have said, 'The LORD is a witness between you and me.'"

# DAVID

avid was a warrior king who first comes into the scene when Samuel anoints him as the next king, after Saul. He was a simple shepherd boy at the time, but the Bible tells us that "the Spirit of the Lord came powerfully upon David from that day on." (1 Samuel 16:13)

David would go on to slay the Philistine warrior Goliath, killing him with God's blessings and a slingshot and stones. After that he became a great warrior for King Saul. He was rewarded with the privilege of marrying Saul's daughter Michal. But Saul eventually became jealous of David, who was popular with the people. Saul ordered David be killed and David and his soldiers became fugitives after that.

After Saul died, David was crowned king.

### GET A CLUE!

What did David do with Goliath's weapons?

– Read: 1 Samuel 17:54 –

He put Goliath's weapons in his own tent.

## KEY WORD(S)

In the Old Testament, *Goliath* was a man's name. Another warrior with the same name is mentioned in a battle recorded in 2 Samuel 21:19. Today, the word *goliath* refers to a person of enormous strength and size as well as to a person or team favored in a contest by huge odds.

▼ *(1 Samuel 16:23)*
*Whenever the spirit from God came on Saul, David would take up his lyre and play.*

## Did You Know?

David loved to praise God by dancing. When the ark of the covenant arrived in Jerusalem, David stripped off his robes and danced for joy. This embarrassed his wife Michal who thought it was undignified behavior for a king.

## ONE MORE THING

David is credited with writing many of the psalms in the Bible. There is no proof of this, but David was well known as a musician who played, sang, and danced to praise God. The psalms are both poems and hymns, and a number of them have been put to music.

# SOLOMON (AND THE QUEEN OF SHEBA)

Solomon followed his father as the next king of Israel. David commanded his son to "Do everything the LORD your God requires. Live the way he wants you to." (1 Kings 2:3) God appeared to Solomon in a dream and promised to give him whatever he wanted. Solomon asked for wisdom to be a good and faithful king. Because he asked for this instead of riches and power, God granted him all three.

Solomon was famous for his wisdom and fairness. People traveled from great distances to listen to his words. The Queen of Sheba, in southern Arabia, arrived in Israel with a grand caravan of gifts. She asked Solomon many questions, eager to learn from him. No matter what the queen asked, Solomon knew the answer. Amazed, the queen declared that the people of Israel were fortunate to have such a wise and glorious king. She praised the God of Israel for the eternal love shown to Solomon. Before the queen began her trip home, Solomon gave her a multitude of gifts to take back to her land.

## KEY WORD(S)

The name, Solomon, probably comes from the Hebrew word, *shalom*, which means "peace." It may also come from the Hebrew word for "replacement," since Solomon was the son born to David and Bathsheba after their first child died.

## GET A CLUE!

What gift did the Queen of Sheba bring to Solomon that was more than anyone had ever given before?

– Read: 1 Kings 10:10 –

She also gave him huge amounts of spices and valuable jewels. No one would ever bring to King Solomon as many spices as the queen of Sheba gave him. "

▲ *This is a decorated panel at the beginning of Proverbs.*

## ONE MORE THING

Because of his legendary wisdom, Solomon is credited with writing many of the proverbs, as well as Song of Songs and Ecclesiastes, although Bible scholars can't be certain.

## Did You Know?

Solomon oversaw the building of the temple in Jerusalem. The temple was God's house on earth and housed the Ark of the Covenant, which held the stone tablets of the Ten Commandments.

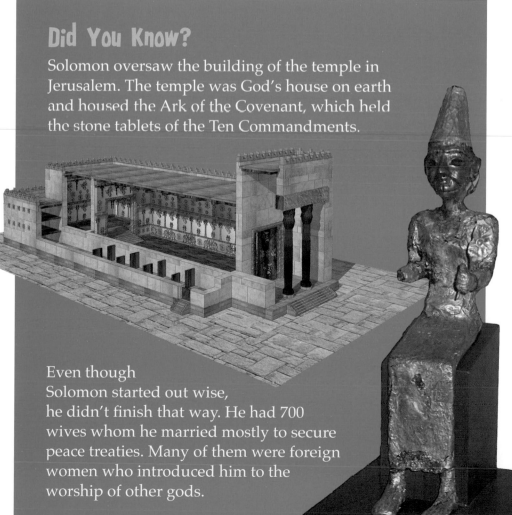

Even though Solomon started out wise, he didn't finish that way. He had 700 wives whom he married mostly to secure peace treaties. Many of them were foreign women who introduced him to the worship of other gods.

# ELIJAH AND ELISHA

**A**round 930 BC, after the death of Solomon, his son, Rehoboam, became king. His poor leadership lead to Israel being divided into two halves. The Northern Kingdom became known as Israel, and the Southern Kingdom as Judah.

God appointed a prophet, Elijah, to serve Israel and defeat the prophets of the pagan god, Baal. Elijah succeeded but had to run for his life from Queen Jezebel. He hid in a mountain. God spoke to him and told him to anoint Elisha as a prophet, which he did. The two of them worked together to bring the Word of God to the people.

Under the guidance of Elijah and Elisha, many of the Israelites who had abandoned God reclaimed their faith.

After Elijah was taken into heaven, Elisha continued to serve God as a mighty prophet until his death.

## KEY WORD(S)
The king of Israel, Ahab, and his wife, Jezebel, encouraged the people to turn from the true God to the Canaanite gods. *Baal* was the name of the god of fertility and storms. God commanded Elijah to destroy the prophets of Baal. In the Hebrew language, the word *ba'al* means "one who possesses," and *Baal* came to mean "lord."

## Did You Know?
The book of Malachi predicts that Elijah will reappear before the day of the Lord (the end times). Because of that prediction and all of his great miracles, Jewish families believed Elijah might be the promised Messiah and would set a place for him at the Passover table.

## ONE MORE THING

When the land dried up because of a terrible drought, God told Elijah to hide in Kerith Ravine. While there, ravens brought him bread and meat in the mornings and evenings, and he found a brook where he could get clean water.

### GET A CLUE!

What happened to Elijah at the end of his life?

– Read: 2 Kings 2:11 –

They kept walking along and talking together. Suddenly there appeared a chariot and horses made of fire. The chariot and horses came between the two men. Then Elijah went up to heaven in a strong wind.

"

After the ruler of Judah was murdered, his mother, Athalia, killed all her grandchildren in order to become queen. The dead king's sister managed to rescue one of her brother's babies, Joash. She hid him for six years until he was brought out of hiding and proclaimed king. Joash was seven years old at the time and the first king of Judah descended from King David.

Joash reigned for forty years, from 837–796 BC. In his early years, he restored the covenant between God and his people. He also oversaw the rebuilding of the Temple of Solomon and reestablished its importance as the center of worship for the Israelites. Joash eventually strayed from God. He gave away all the temple treasures as a bribe to protect the city of Jerusalem. His own officials later killed him.

Josiah was another king who began his rule as a child. He was crowned at the age of eight, after his father, King Amon, died. Josiah, like Joash, oversaw further renovation of

the temple. The workers uncovered a holy book and brought it to Josiah. He recognized it as the Book of the Law, which contained the laws of God by which the people were supposed to live. Josiah called together all the leaders of Judah and Jerusalem and read aloud from the Book. The people renewed their covenant with God once again. Josiah remained a righteous and honest king for his thirty-one years, from 641–609 BC. He was killed in a battle and sadly, the son who was crowned king after Josiah turned the people from God once again.

## KEY WORD(S)

The first five books of the Hebrew Bible are known as the *Pentateuch* ("five books" or "five scrolls"). It contains the *Torah*, or law. *Torah* means, "guide, teach, instruction." The Book of the Law is thought to be the book of Deuteronomy, the fifth book of the Pentateuch.

## GET A CLUE!

Joash was orphaned as a baby. Who taught him how to be a good king?

– Read: Matthew 13:55 –

Joash did what was right in the eyes of the Lᴏʀᴅ. Joash lived that way as long as Jehoiada the priest was teaching him. **"**

## ONE MORE THING

Josiah died from a battle wound. He was trying to block the armies of Egypt's Pharaoh Necho from helping the Assyrian army.

▶ *A plaque fragment of Necho II*

## Did You Know?

The temple that Joash repaired was the temple built by Solomon. Joash commanded that any money brought into the temple not be spent on items but be used to pay the workers doing repairs.

**M**esopotamia is a region in western Asia. Mesopotamia is where some of the greatest developments in human history occurred, including the invention of the wheel and the developments of math, astronomy, and modern agriculture. The word Mesopotamia can be roughly translated as "land between the rivers" because it included both the Tigris and Euphrates rivers.

## ASSYRIA

The Assyrian Empire was at its height beginning after the time of David and Solomon, around 934–612 BC. The capital of this kingdom was Nineveh. In about 722 BC Assyria overran Israel and destroyed the ten tribes living there. Their people were dispersed and integrated into other cultures.

▶ *The tomb of Cyrus the Great is a monument located near Pasargadae, Iran.*

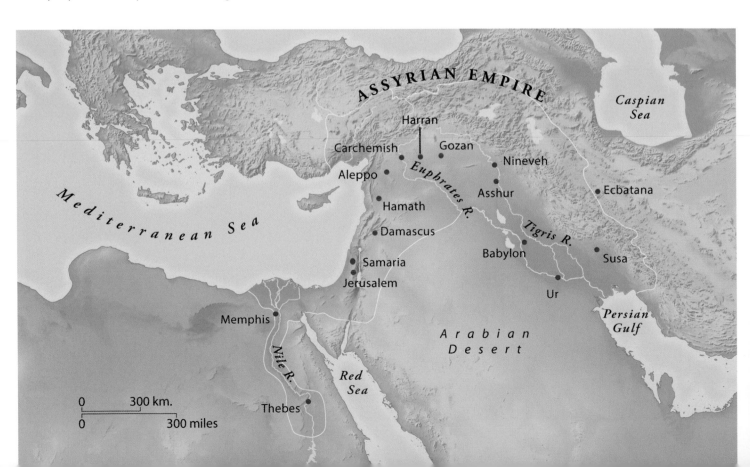

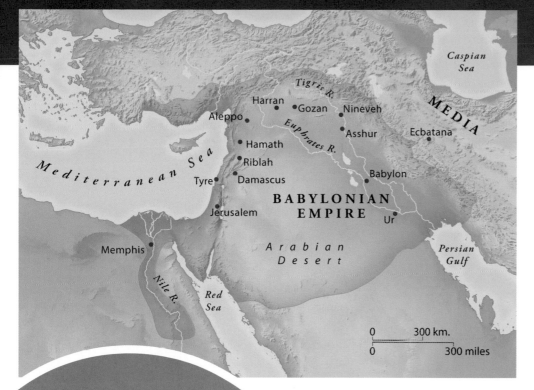

## BABYLON

The Babylonian Empire stretched from the Persian Gulf to the Mediterranean Sea to the Red Sea. Babylon conquered the Assyrian Empire, which had existed in that region before. Babylon was at its height during the time of Nebuchadnezzar (605–562 BC). Nebuchadnezzar was responsible for the destruction of Jerusalem. It was during the time of the Babylonian Empire that the story of Daniel takes place.

## PERSIA

Cyrus the Great was the first ruler of Persia (around 559 BC) to have significant military victories. He conquered the Medes and Babylon. He freed the Jewish captives in Babylon and allowed them to return to Jerusalem. The Persian Empire only lasted a few hundred years. It was defeated by the Greek army of Alexander the Great around 330 BC. It was during the time of the Persian Empire that the story of Esther takes place.

▲ *The Hanging Gardens are considered one of the Seven Wonders of the Ancient World, though they no longer exist. Nebuchadnezzar built it for his queen who was homesick for the beautiful mountains where she was born.*

# QUEEN ESTHER

Almost 600 years before Jesus, the Jewish people were defeated in war. Many of them were taken to other countries in exile, almost like prisoners. Esther grew up as a Jewish exile in the land of Persia. Years before, many Jews had been captured and brought to Persia during the Babylonian Empire. Mordecai was Esther's relative and served as her guardian, since she was an orphan.

**GET A CLUE!**

When Xerxes chose Esther as his new queen, what did he give her?

– Read: Esther 2:9 –
Right away he provided her with her beauty care and special food. ,,

Xerxes, the king, was looking for a new queen, so beautiful young women of the kingdom were brought to him. Xerxes chose Esther, not knowing that she was Jewish.

Haman was the king's most honored advisor. Haman hated the Jews and devised a plan to get rid of them. He convinced Xerxes to rid the empire of the Jewish people.

Mordecai persuaded Esther to ask the king to spare her life and the lives of her people. Esther risked her life to speak to the king and then confronted Haman. When Xerxes discovered that Haman had tricked him and planned to take the life of his queen and all the Jews, he had Haman and his sons executed.

## Did You Know?

Xerxes ruled over a huge kingdom, which spread from India in the southwest to the borders of Greece in the northeast. Persia is now known as the country of Iran. This is Persepolis, the ceremonial capital during the reign of Xerxes.

## KEY WORD(S)

The name, *Esther*, comes from the Persian word for "star." Esther's name might also come from the name of the Babylonian goddess, *Ishtar*, which means "Queen of Heaven." Her name in Hebrew was *Haddasah*, which means "myrtle," a type of tree.

## ONE MORE THING

*Purim* is celebrated by Jews every year on the 14th day of the Jewish month of *Adar*, which usually falls around March 14th. It is a day of feasting and joy, celebrating the time when the Jewish people in exile were set free from their enemies.

# THE MAJOR PROPHETS

Old Testament prophets spoke on behalf of God. They announced God's plans for the people of Israel, warned them what would happen if they strayed from their obedience to God, and promised a future when God would reign over the entire world. There are major prophets and minor prophets. The books called the Major Prophets are longer than the Minor Prophets. Isaiah, Jeremiah, Ezekiel, and Daniel are the four Major Prophets.

▲ Isaiah lived in the 8th century BC. He had a vision of God in which God asked, "Whom shall I send?" Isaiah replied, "Here I am. Send me." (Isaiah 6:8)

### GET A CLUE!

What did God ask Ezekiel to eat before he began his role as a prophet?

– Read: Ezekiel 3:1 –

The LORD said to me, "Son of man, eat what is in front of you. Eat this scroll. Then go and speak to the people of Israel."

## Did You Know?

John the Baptist quotes from Isaiah (Isaiah 40:3): "As it is written in the book of the words of Isaiah the prophet: 'A voice of one calling in the wilderness, "Prepare the way for the Lord, make straight paths for him."'" (Luke 3:4–6)

The definition for the Hebrew, *prophet*, is "spokesman," or "speaker." A prophet was not a fortune-teller. Fortune-tellers called upon evil spirits and the dead, which was forbidden by God.

▶ *Jeremiah was the son of a priest. As a prophet, he spoke to the Jews in Judea and to those who had been captured by foreign empires and forced to live in exile. Jeremiah is known as "the weeping prophet" because of the difficult times he endured.*

▶ *Ezekiel's message was meant for the Jewish captives living in Babylonia.*

▶ *Daniel was captured as a boy and exiled in Babylon. His mission was to the Jewish exiles as well as the Gentile (non-Jewish) kings.*

Jeremiáš    Ezechiel    Daniel

## ONE MORE THING

Jeremiah is believed to be the writer of the book of Lamentations. The name comes from a Hebrew word that means "dirge" or "lament." A lament shows grief and sadness. Lamentations is about the sadness of the Jewish exiles in foreign lands.

# DANIEL

ebuchadnezzar, the king of Babylon, conquered Jerusalem in 605 BC. This resulted in the capture and exile of many Jewish people. Many of the exiled men were trained to serve in the palace. One of these young men was Daniel. He could understand dreams and visions, which made him valuable to the kings and leaders. He interpreted dreams for Nebuchadnezzar, which led the king to praise the God of Israel.

Many in the king's court hated Daniel for his abilities. They tricked the new king, Darius, into sentencing Daniel to death. Darius reluctantly had Daniel thrown into a den of lions, but prayed that Daniel's God would save him. The next morning, the king found Daniel safe and alive. The men who had falsely accused him were thrown into the den and devoured by the lions instead.

## ONE MORE THING

The book of Daniel contains the story of three Jewish men thrown into a fiery furnace because they refused to turn away from God. Their faith saved Shadrach, Meshach, and Abednego, which is the reason Nebuchadnezzar began to believe in the God of Israel.

## Did You Know?

Daniel observed a kosher diet, which had strict rules about what kinds of food could be eaten and how it must be prepared. As a result, Daniel and his friends were healthier than others working in the palace.

## GET A CLUE!

What qualifications did the Jewish exiles have to have in order to serve in the palace?

– Read: Daniel 1:3 –

He wanted nobles and men from the royal family. He was looking for young men who were healthy and handsome. They had to be able to learn anything. They had to be well educated. They had to have the ability to understand new things quickly and easily. "

## KEY WORD(S)

At a palace feast during Belshazzar's reign, the fingers of a human hand appeared and wrote on the wall: *Mene, Mene, Tekel, Parsin.* The meaning of the specific words is "count," "weigh," "divide." Daniel was able to put the meanings together. Their message: the king's days had come to an end and his kingdom would be divided and given away. That night, Belshazzar was assassinated.

# JONAH

God wanted to send a prophet named Jonah to preach to the people in Nineveh, a major city in the Assyrian empire. But the Assyrians were longtime enemies of the Jewish people and Jonah did not think they deserved to hear the word of God and to be saved from destruction.

So, Jonah ran in the other direction. He headed west, boarded a ship, and hoped that God wouldn't notice. God responded by sending a mighty wind that created a raging storm. The sailors on board were terrified. Jonah admitted that the storm raged because of his disobedience so, with nothing else to do to save themselves, they threw Jonah overboard. Immediately, the sea became calm.

A huge fish swallowed Jonah. For three days, Jonah prayed for God to set him free. Finally, the fish spit him onto dry land. Again, God told Jonah to go to Nineveh and preach. This time, Jonah listened. Surprisingly, the king and all the people asked for forgiveness and turned from their evil ways. God did not destroy their city.

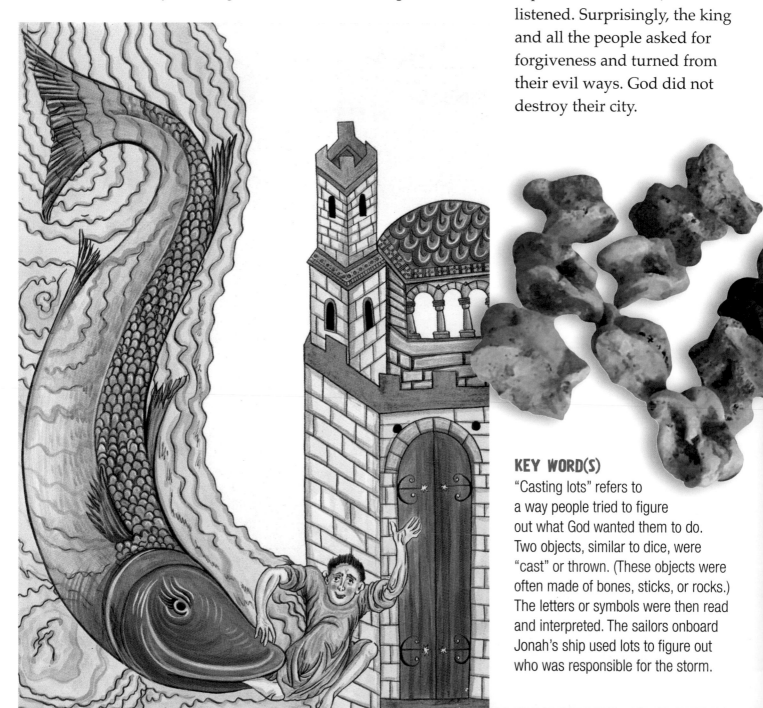

## KEY WORD(S)

"Casting lots" refers to a way people tried to figure out what God wanted them to do. Two objects, similar to dice, were "cast" or thrown. (These objects were often made of bones, sticks, or rocks.) The letters or symbols were then read and interpreted. The sailors onboard Jonah's ship used lots to figure out who was responsible for the storm.

## ONE MORE THING

People of the Jewish faith
read the story of Jonah on
Yom Kippur, the Day of Atonement.
This is a national day of repentance, which is when the people ask
God for forgiveness.

## Did You Know?

Nineveh was an ancient Assyrian city near modern-day
Mosul in northern Iraq. This is an artist's depiction of what
Nineveh looked like around the time of Jonah.

## GET A CLUE!

What was Jonah's reaction
to God forgiving the people
of Nineveh?

– Read: Jonah 4:1–3 –

But to Jonah this seemed very
wrong. He became angry. He
prayed to the Lord. Here is what
Jonah said to him. "Lord, isn't
this exactly what I thought would
happen when I was still at home?
That is what I tried to prevent
by running away to Tarshish.
I knew that you are gracious.
You are tender and kind. You are
slow to get angry. You are full
of love. You are a God who takes
pity on people. You don't want
to destroy them. Lord, take
away my life. I'd rather
die than live."

”

55

# THE MINOR PROPHETS

The twelve minor prophets are Hosea, Joel, Amos, Obadiah, Jonah, Micah, Nahum, Habakkuk, Zephaniah, Haggai, Zechariah, and Malachi. In ancient Judaism, the stories of these prophets were written on scrolls. Hosea is the longest, with fourteen chapters, and Obadiah is the shortest with only one. Malachi, the final book in the Old Testament, includes God's promise to "bring peace between children and their parents." (Malachi 4:6)

Each prophetic book includes clues to the prophet's identity, and "oracles," or speeches often written as poetry. The first six minor prophets focus on the sins and crimes of the Israelites, while the rest are more concerned with resolutions that would unite the people under God's authority once again.

## GET A CLUE!

What did Micah say would one day come from the city of Bethlehem?

– Read: Micah 5:2 –

But out of you will come for me a ruler over Israel.

56

## ONE MORE THING

Other cultures had people they believed had divine knowledge, similar to the major and minor prophets who brought God's word to his people. Some of those cultures even built temples dedicated to these people. One of the most famous is the Oracle of Delphi, who lived in a temple built for Apollo, the sun god. Believers would come from far and wide to ask questions of the oracle, hoping for answers about their futures.

▲ *Temple of the Oracle of Delphi.*

## Did You Know?

The prophets called for justice, or fairness, in the governing of and treatment of all people. They challenged the people of Israel to care for the widow, the orphan, and the stranger. Widows and orphans were very likely poor, because they had no one to support them.

## KEY WORD(S)

A *scroll* was made up of different pages glued together at the edges. One page of the scroll could be read, then wound up to allow the viewing of the next page. Some scrolls had wooden rollers to make it easier to roll up.

The Roman Empire was the largest political and social structure in the west. Its power lasted from about 27 BC to AD 395 when it grew too big to be ruled by one central power. It was split into east and west. At the time of Jesus' birth, it included parts of the Middle East, North Africa, Greece, Italy, Spain, France, and some parts of modern-day Austria, Switzerland, and Germany.

Judea was a Roman province that included Judea, Samaria, and Idumea and other parts of the former kingdoms of Israel. The province was ruled by a Roman prefect, kind of like a governor, at the time of Jesus. As time went on, leadership and titles changed.

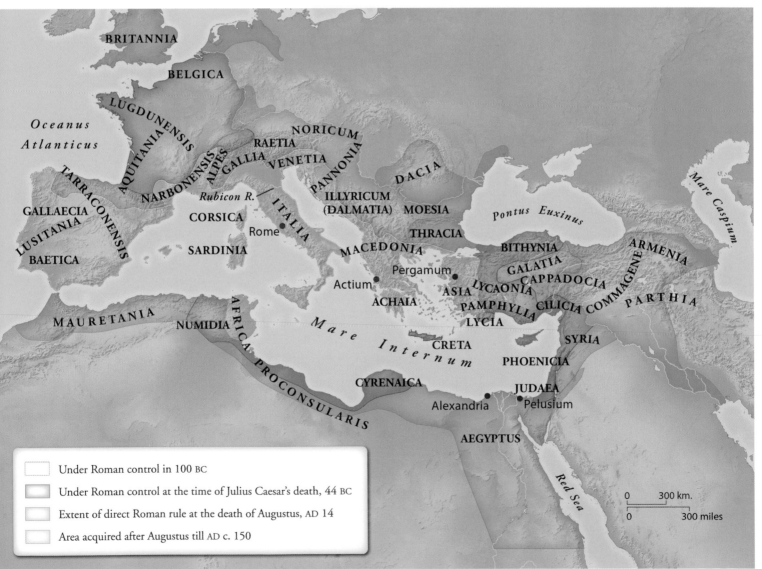

Under Roman control in 100 BC

Under Roman control at the time of Julius Caesar's death, 44 BC

Extent of direct Roman rule at the death of Augustus, AD 14

Area acquired after Augustus till AD c. 150

▲ *The Roman Empire expanded greatly between 100 BC and AD 150.*

## JERUSALEM

The Romans invaded Jerusalem in 63 BC. Jerusalem in the first century AD was like other Roman cities. It had a theater and a hippodrome where chariot races took place. During the time of Jesus, the temple that Herod rebuilt stood on the Temple Mount. Later, the Jews would rebel against Roman rule, and the temple would be destroyed. It would never be rebuilt.

## EARLY CHRISTIANS AND THE SPREAD OF CHRISTIANITY

Christianity spread quickly in part because it was so easy for teachers to travel on Roman roads. The religion also may have appealed to non-Jews that the apostles met when some rules about cleanliness and eating were relaxed.

## JEWS IN ROMAN TIMES

For the most part, Jews lived peacefully throughout the Roman Empire. They were allowed to worship as they liked in Rome and Judea. However, in Judea, the governors were often insensitive to Jewish customs. The people were also highly taxed to pay both the Roman Empire and King Herod. This led to poverty, hunger, and debt. This is why Jesus often spoke about these issues. The Jewish people were ready for a leader who would show them love and care.

At the time, many Jews in Judea were likely to be farmers. Most Jewish families worked to sustain themselves. However, there were also merchants due to the trade routes, craftsmen, doctors, and religious and business leaders.

# MARY AND JOSEPH

The Bible doesn't say much about Jesus' parents, Mary and Joseph. We don't know how they met, how old they were when Jesus was born, or how they died. These facts aren't most important to the story.

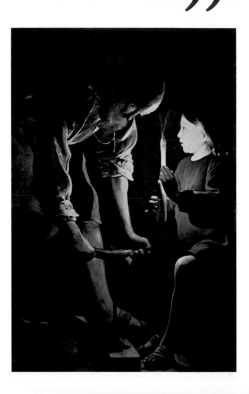

We do know that Mary was engaged to be married to Joseph when the angel, Gabriel, appeared to her and told her she would give birth to Jesus, God's son.
When Joseph learned that Mary was pregnant, he decided to divorce her. An angel appeared to Joseph in a dream and convinced him that the baby she carried was God's son. Joseph accepted his chosen role as the earthly father of Jesus.
Mary is mentioned throughout the life of Jesus. She comes to him when he is teaching in the temple and is present as he is crucified.

## GET A CLUE!

What was Joseph's profession?

– Read: Matthew 13:55 –

"Isn't this the carpenter's son? Isn't his mother's name Mary, and aren't his brothers James, Joseph, Simon and Judas?"

## Did You Know?

Engagement was a financial agreement between a man and a woman. It usually lasted a year. Often, marriages were arranged and the man and woman did not know each other before the engagement. This was a time for them to get to know each other and prepare their new household.

◄ *A twelfth-century psalter shows the Tree of Jesse, including King David, and ending with Jesus.*

## KEY WORD(S)

The announcement by the angel Gabriel to Mary that she would give birth to the son of God is referred to as the *Annunciation*. In general terms, *annunciation* means "an act or instance of announcing or proclamation." But this word is most often used in reference to Mary. Many Christians observe the Feast of the Annunciation. Many artistic works show this event. In fact, so many have been created that a work of art showing the annunciation is sometimes itself called an Annunciation.

## ONE MORE THING

Joseph is the one through whom Jesus' lineage is traced. It was important to show that King David was listed in Jesus' family tree. One of the titles for Jesus is the "Son of David." In the Bible, the list of descendants always starts with the males. Jesus' list includes the names of several women, which was unusual for the time.

After Jesus' birth, he had a number of unlikely visitors.

A group of magi (wise men) was led to Bethlehem by following a star.

An angel appeared to a group of shepherds tending their sheep in the fields. Shepherds lived with their flocks because they needed constant protection and care. Shepherds were not highly regarded but very necessary to the running of the nation. They would be dirty and rough, and not normally welcome to visit at the birth of a baby. They left their sheep and hurried to town to see the baby the angels had told them about.

Eight days after Jesus' birth, his parents presented him at the temple in Jerusalem. While in Jerusalem, a man named Simeon searched for the baby. The Holy Spirit had revealed to Simeon that he would not die before the Messiah came to the world. Simeon held baby Jesus and praised God for keeping the promise.

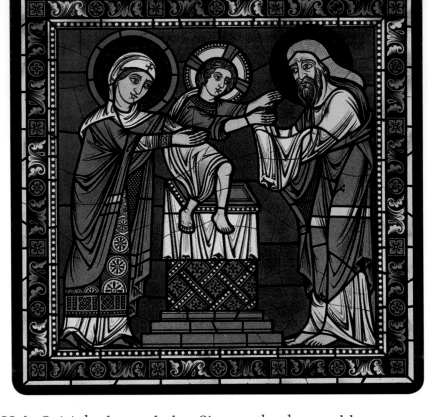

A prophet named Anna lived in the temple where she worshiped, fasted, and prayed. When she saw Jesus and his parents, she also thanked God and told others that this was the promised Son of God.

## GET A CLUE!

Where did the magi find Jesus?

– Read: Matthew 2:11 –

On coming to the house, they saw the child with his mother Mary, and they bowed down and worshiped him. Then they opened their treasures and presented him with gifts of gold, frankincense and myrrh.

"

## ONE MORE THING

In the Bible, angels are often messengers of God. They bring news to people about God's plans, as they did to Mary, Joseph, and the shepherds. The Hebrew word for angel means "messenger."

## KEY WORD(S)

*Magi* comes from a Latin word, *magus*, which could refer to a magician or sorcerer. It also refers to a priest in the Zoroastrian religion of ancient Persia. The magi who traveled from the east to see Jesus were most likely priests or astrologers, people trained to read the meaning of the placement of the planets and stars. The magi are often shown as three kings, although there is no mention in the Bible of the number, and they weren't kings. They would have traveled with a large caravan to carry the gifts and other provisions such as tents and food.

## Did You Know?

Several of the most important people in the Bible served as shepherds at some point in their lives: Abel, Moses, Abraham, Isaac, Jacob, Esau, Rachel, Moses, Aaron, David, and Amos. Jesus is referred to as "The Good Shepherd." John the Baptist called Jesus "the Lamb of God."

# HEROD THE GREAT

Herod the Great descended from Esau, the brother of Jacob. He was considered to be Jewish, although he may not have practiced his faith. The Romans, who ruled Judah (northern Israel) in the time of Jesus, declared him "King of the Jews." Devout Jews did not approve of his lavish lifestyle and brutal rule. He killed anyone who opposed him.

When the magi came through Jerusalem following the star, they asked where to find "the one who has been born king of the Jews." (2 Matthew 2) This greatly disturbed Herod because he wanted to be the only king. He asked the teachers of Jewish law to confirm the magi's quest. They did, quoting from the prophet Micah, who had said that the child would be born in Bethlehem.

Herod asked the magi to report back to him after they found the baby. He said he wanted to worship the new king. But the magi were warned in a dream that Herod was up to no good. After finding the baby Jesus, they returned to their country by a different route.

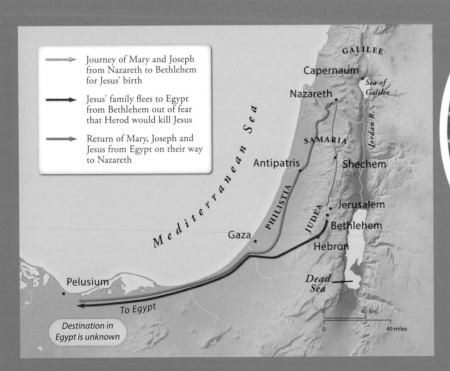

Journey of Mary and Joseph from Nazareth to Bethlehem for Jesus' birth

Jesus' family flees to Egypt from Bethlehem out of fear that Herod would kill Jesus

Return of Mary, Joseph and Jesus from Egypt on their way to Nazareth

GALILEE
Capernaum
Sea of Galilee
Nazareth
Jordan R.
Mediterranean Sea
SAMARIA
Antipatris
Shechem
PHILISTIA
JUDEA
Jerusalem
Gaza
Bethlehem
Hebron
Pelusium
Dead Sea
To Egypt
Destination in Egypt is unknown

0       40 km.
0       40 miles

## Did You Know?

Herod was furious that the magi had tricked him. He ordered all the males living in Bethlehem under the age of two years to be killed. He believed that in doing this, he would get rid of any chances of a new king taking his place. But Joseph, Mary, and Jesus escaped to Egypt where they lived until Herod died.

## GET A CLUE!

Who else besides Herod was frightened that the magi came to visit the newborn king of the Jews?

– Read: Matthew 2:3 –

When King Herod heard this he was disturbed, and all Jerusalem with him. **"**

◄ *A model of Herod's palace in Jerusalem. This is where Jesus appeared before Herod Antipas.*

## KEY WORD(S)

Remove the last letter in Herod's name and you have a clue as to the meaning of the word. The name Herod means, "hero," as well as "warrior," or "song of the hero."

## ONE MORE THING

Herod the Great oversaw the rebuilding of the Second Temple in Jerusalem. This became one of the ancient world's largest and fanciest temples. However, he also built temples for worship of pagan gods and rulers, including the emperor, Augustus. Jesus often taught in the temple.

# JOHN THE BAPTIST

A priest named Zechariah and his wife, Elizabeth, wanted a child, but they were too old to have a baby. The angel Gabriel appeared to Zechariah and told him that Elizabeth would give birth to a son. This child would grow up to be holy and prepare the people for the coming of the Messiah. The baby was born and Zechariah named him John, as Gabriel had told him to do.

John began his ministry in the wilderness preparing for Jesus. He told people that the Messiah would soon arrive, just as other prophets had said. He called for people to turn away from sin and be prepared for the coming of this Messiah. He baptized those who believed what he said. But some people were angered by John's message and looked for a way to kill him.

John understood who Jesus was the moment he saw him. Jesus asked John to baptize him with water from the Jordan River, which he did.

John's enemies later found a way to have him killed. Jesus deeply grieved for the death of his friend and cousin.

◀ *John chose to live a simple life in the wilderness, preaching about Jesus' coming.*

## GET A CLUE!

How did John dress and what did he eat?

– Read: Matthew 3:4 –

John's clothes were made of camel's hair, and he had a leather belt around his waist. His food was locusts and wild honey.

**"**

## KEY WORD(S)

*Messiah* comes from the Hebrew word, *mashiach*, which means "Messiah," or "anointed one." The Greek word for Messiah is *Christos*, or "Christ." A prophet anointed a new king with oil as a sign that this person had been chosen by God.

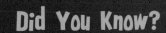

## Did You Know?

Before Christianity, water was used by many religions as a symbol of the cleansing of the soul. Baptism was often a requirement before a person could enter worship or a holy place. Today, Christians are baptized as a sign that they belong to Jesus Christ. Baptize means "immerse." Some churches believe that a person being baptized must be completely submerged in water, while in others, water is poured on the head of the individual.

## ONE MORE THING

Herod (not Herod the Great) wanted to kill John the Baptist because he had criticized him for doing something bad. Herod feared John's followers, so he threw him into jail instead. John was later beheaded at the request of Herod's daughter (or possibly stepdaughter). She pleased him by dancing for him at his birthday party. He told her she could have whatever she wanted. She requested the head of John the Baptist on a platter, under the influence of her mother.

# JESUS

We don't know too much about how Jesus grew up but we can imagine it was similar to other Jewish children of the time. His father, Joseph, is said to have been a carpenter. It is possible that he had brothers and sisters, though not all believers agree on this.

For those who believed that Jesus was the son of God, he was the promised Messiah that prophets had told about thousands of years before his birth. For those who didn't believe, he was often thought of as a religious teacher who was stirring up discontent among the people.

## ONE MORE THING

Josephus, a Jewish Roman historian who was born around the time of Jesus' death wrote about Jesus. He said, "At this time there was a wise man called Jesus, and his conduct was good, and he was known to be virtuous. And many people from among the Jews and the other nations became his disciples … they believed he was the Messiah, concerning whom the Prophets have recounted wonders."

## GET A CLUE!

Who led Jesus into the wilderness to be tempted in the first place?

– Read: Luke 4:1 –

Jesus, full of the Holy Spirit, left the Jordan and was led by the Spirit into the wilderness. **"**

Jesus is the English translation of a Greek name which in turn comes from the Aramaic name *Yeshua*. The name *Joshua* also comes from this name. Roughly, it means "the Lord is salvation." Christ is from the Greek word *Christos*. This is a translation of the Hebrew word *Masiah*, which means "Anointed One." So, Jesus is called the Christ because he is thought to be the Hebrew people's promised Messiah.

◀ *The Chi Rho monogram. Chi and Rho are the first two letters in the Greek word Christos.*

# Did You Know?

According to the Bible, here are a few events on the timeline of Jesus' life:

- At about 12 years old his parents lose him on a visit to the temple in Jerusalem and later find him talking to religious scholars.
- Baptized in the Jordan River by John the Baptist, his relative
- Spends forty days and nights in the desert, being tempted by the devil
- At about 30 years old Jesus begins his public ministry and gathers his disciples.
- Jesus performed miracles such as healing diseases and casting out demons.
- Jesus tells stories called parables that help show the people how they should treat each other.
- At about 33 years old Jesus is betrayed by Judas, one of his disciples.
- Jesus is brought before Jewish and Roman officials and sentenced to death.
- He is crucified and dies.
- Jesus is raised from the dead and appears to some disciples.
- Jesus ascends into heaven.

# GALILEE

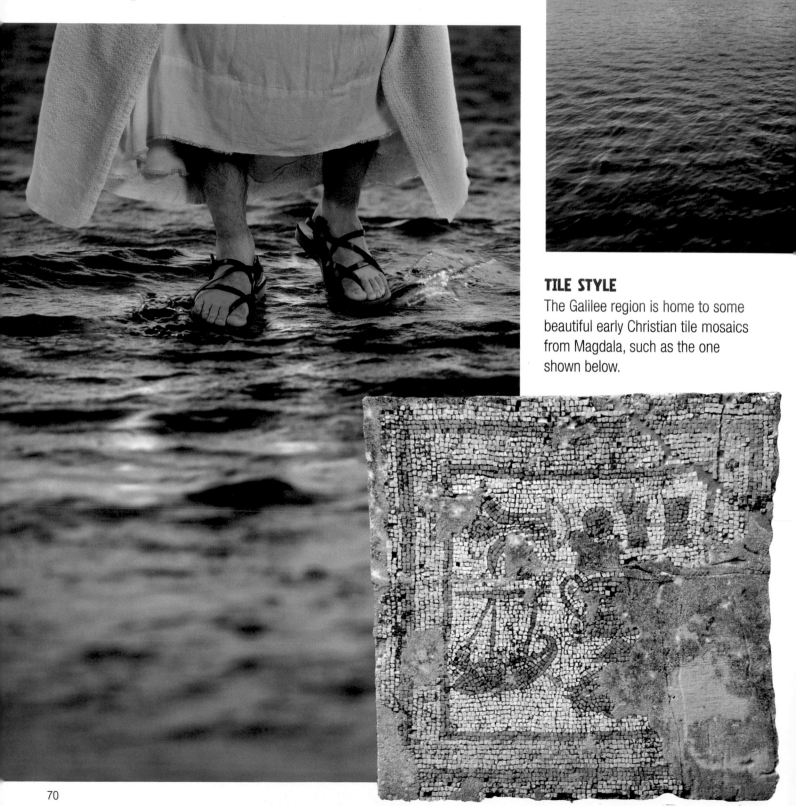

**M**uch of Jesus' public ministry happened around the Sea of Galilee, now known as Lake Kinneret. At the water's edge, he called four of his disciples. In the towns around it, he taught and transformed people. And on the surface of the water itself, Jesus performed miracles.

## TILE STYLE

The Galilee region is home to some beautiful early Christian tile mosaics from Magdala, such as the one shown below.

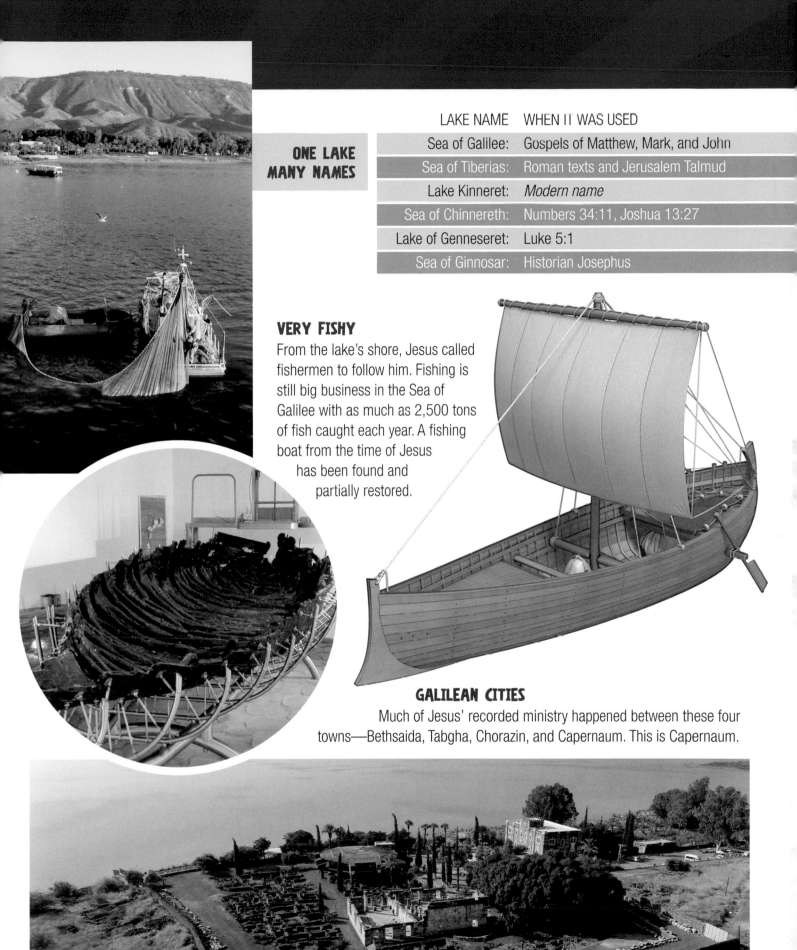

### ONE LAKE MANY NAMES

| LAKE NAME | WHEN IT WAS USED |
|---|---|
| Sea of Galilee: | Gospels of Matthew, Mark, and John |
| Sea of Tiberias: | Roman texts and Jerusalem Talmud |
| Lake Kinneret: | *Modern name* |
| Sea of Chinnereth: | Numbers 34:11, Joshua 13:27 |
| Lake of Genneseret: | Luke 5:1 |
| Sea of Ginnosar: | Historian Josephus |

### VERY FISHY

From the lake's shore, Jesus called fishermen to follow him. Fishing is still big business in the Sea of Galilee with as much as 2,500 tons of fish caught each year. A fishing boat from the time of Jesus has been found and partially restored.

### GALILEAN CITIES

Much of Jesus' recorded ministry happened between these four towns—Bethsaida, Tabgha, Chorazin, and Capernaum. This is Capernaum.

# THE TWELVE DISCIPLES

At the beginning of Jesus' ministry, he chose twelve people to be a special team. Everyone who follows Jesus is his disciple, but those chosen by him are known as the Twelve Disciples. Sometimes they are called "apostles." These men traveled everywhere with him and learned firsthand all that Jesus had to teach about his Father. This was so that they could continue to teach and share the message later.

The disciples were Simon (Peter), Andrew, James (son of Zebedee), John, Phillip, Thaddeus (Jude/Judas), Bartholomew (Nathaniel), Thomas, James (Levi), Matthew, Simon (the Canaanite), and Judas Iscariot. Several were fishermen, one was a tax collector, and one was a thief.

During his ministry on earth, Jesus had many other disciples, including women. In the book of Luke, Jesus asked seventy followers to spread God's Word from town to town. It was through the disciples that Jesus' message of the good news of the gospel began to find its way into the world.

## Did You Know?

Simon, whose name Jesus changed to Peter is mentioned nearly 200 times, twice as often as the rest of the disciples put together. He was the first to recognize Jesus as the Son of God. He tried to walk on water during a storm, denied Jesus after his trial, and was the first of the twelve to enter the empty tomb on the first Easter morning. After his resurrection, Jesus appeared to the disciples on the beach and told Peter to "feed his sheep." (John 21:15–29) Peter was the first leader of the early church.

▲ *The disciples prepare to go out and spread the gospel.*
*Judas has been replaced by Matthias.*

## ONE MORE THING

After Judas died, he was replaced by a new apostle, but not until after Jesus rose from the dead. The other disciples prayed about it in the upper room of the house in which they gathered. Three men were chosen, and lots were cast to decide which man would be the next disciple. Matthias was the one.

### KEY WORD(S)

The word *disciple* comes from the Greek word, *mathetes*, which means "pupil," "student," "one who learns." The word *discipline* comes from this same Greek word. *Apostle* means "one who is sent," because they are given the power of one who sends them.

◄ *A rabbi and his pupils.*
*(Detail of artist rendering)*

### GET A CLUE!

Which disciples were brothers?

– Read: Matthew 4:18–21 –

As Jesus was walking beside the Sea of Galilee, he saw two brothers, Simon called Peter and his brother Andrew. They were casting a net into the lake, for they were fishermen … Going on from there, he saw two other brothers, James son of Zebedee and his brother John. They were in a boat with their father Zebedee, preparing their nets. **"**

# LAZARUS, MARY, AND MARTHA

Lazarus and his two sisters, Mary and Martha, lived in a suburb of Jerusalem called Bethany. The family considered Jesus a good friend and welcomed Jesus and the disciples into their home. It was a great honor to have Jesus, a respected rabbi and teacher, in their home.

The two sisters were very different from each other. In one story in the Bible Mary wanted to take in every word that Jesus said. As he talked, she sat at his feet where the men sat.

Martha did not sit, but busied herself preparing the meal and making sure that her guests felt welcome. It angered her to see Mary sitting rather than helping. She complained to Jesus, who told her not to be so anxious. Listening to the Word of God was a better choice.

In another story, Lazarus became seriously ill. Mary and Martha sent a message to Jesus to come immediately. By the time he arrived in Bethany, two days later, Lazarus had died. Saddened, the sisters joined Jesus outside Lazarus' tomb.

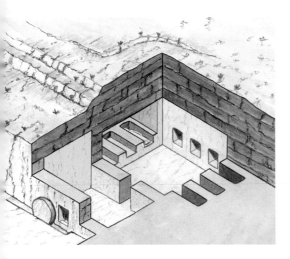

Jesus shared their sadness and wept. Then he said, "I am the resurrection and the life." He commanded Lazarus to come out from the tomb. To the shock of everyone, Lazarus, still wrapped in his burial clothes, walked out.

## ONE MORE THING

Lazarus was not the only person who Jesus raised from the dead. He raised the son of a widow (Luke 7:11–15) and the daughter of Jairus (Luke 8:55). The Old Testament prophets, Elijah and Elisha, brought back several people from the dead. And Peter raised Dorcas (Tabitha) after Pentecost. (Acts 9:36–43)

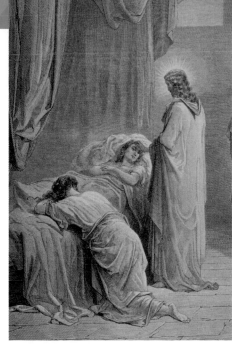

▶ *Jesus and the daughter of Jairus.*

## KEY WORD(S)

Jesus is often called *teacher* or *rabbi*. In Hebrew, a rabbi is one who is trained to teach the Jewish law. Jesus, a Jew, learned about the law by going to the temple when he was growing up. A rabbi was a respected position, and calling Jesus "rabbi" showed the power he had in the eyes of man.

## Did You Know?

In the first century, most people were not buried in graves or cremated. Bodies were covered with preserving oils and wrapped in cloth. They were laid inside caves cut into rock walls or built with stone. A large stone covered the entrance.

After a year or so, family members would go back into the tomb. They would place the bones of the deceased in a stone box (called an "ossuary"), which would remain in the family tomb alongside other ossuaries. The tomb of Lazarus would have been very similar to the one in which Jesus' body was placed after his death.

┌─────────────────────────────┐
│ ── GET A CLUE! ── │
│ How did Jesus respond when │
│ he knew Lazarus had died? │
│ │
│ – Read: John 11:35 – │
│ Jesus wept. │
└─────────────────────────────┘
"

75

# PETER

Peter was born in Bethsaida, along the northern shore of the Sea of Galilee. He was a fisherman who lived as an adult in the village of Capernaum. At the time, his name was Simon, son of Jonah.

One day, Jesus was teaching in the area. He asked the owner of a fishing boat to take him out on the water so he could address the crowd. It was Peter's boat. After hearing Jesus speak and seeing a miracle, Peter and other fishermen, including Peter's brother Andrew, left their jobs and followed Jesus.

Peter was one of Jesus' closest friends. It was to Jesus that Peter walked on water. He witnessed Jesus bring a young girl back to life. Peter was also the first disciple to declare that Jesus is the Son of God. However, Peter is also remembered for denying that he was a follower of Jesus three times before the crucifixion.

Peter went on to become one of the early church leaders.

## ONE MORE THING
There are two letters in the Bible from Peter. First and 2 Peter are words of advice to believers in what is now western Turkey. Many scholars doubt that these were actually written by Peter, since the language is too refined for a common fisherman. It is possible that a more learned friend helped him.

◄ *The illuminated letter P at the beginning of 1 Peter in the 1417 AD Latin Bible.*

► *St. Peter's Basilica is one of the most recognizable churches in the world and is the traditional burial site of Peter.*

**GET A CLUE!**

Who did Peter injure during a conflict with an official in Gethsemane?

– Read: John 18:10 –
Simon Peter had a sword and pulled it out. He struck the high priest's slave and cut off his right ear. The slave's name was Malchus.

99

## Did You Know?

Like other Christians of the time, Peter was persecuted and eventually killed by the Romans. He was crucified. But because he felt unworthy to die in exactly the same way as his Lord, he asked to be crucified upside down.

## KEY WORD(S)

Jesus renamed Peter because he would be the "rock I will build my church on." *Peter* comes from the Greek name *Petros*, which means "rock." His name in Aramaic, the language of Jesus' day, was *Cephas*, which roughly means "rock" or "stone."

# JERUSALEM

Some amazing discoveries have been made in what is modern Jerusalem. For example, archaeologists have found evidence of a 7,000-year-old settlement there. Jerusalem has gone by many names—Urusalim, Salem, Jebus, and Moriah among them. The name Jerusalem is first used in the book of Joshua.

## MOUNT OF OLIVES

A major geographic feature, the Mount of Olives plays a big role in the Bible as well. Zechariah prophesied about it, Ezekiel had a vision about it, David fled there, and Jesus crossed it into Bethany. Jesus rested, taught, and prayed among its olive trees. After the Last Supper, Jesus and his disciples went to pray in the Garden of Gethsemane. Some of the olive trees in Gethsemane have been found to be 1,000 years old.

▶ *Today, the Dome of the Rock, a Muslim mosque, sits on the Temple Mount, its gold top highlighting the Jerusalem skyline.*

## THE TEMPLE MOUNT

King Solomon built the First Temple at the place where Abraham brought Isaac to be sacrificed—Mount Moriah. After Solomon's temple was destroyed, the Second Temple was built by King Herod on the same spot.

## WALLS AND GATES

The original walls surrounding the Old City were for protection. Today, the walls stretch nearly three miles in length and reach up to 50 feet at the highest point.

◄ *Part of the wall that surrounded the Second Temple had been standing since before Jesus was born. Recognized as the only surviving portion of the temple, Jews respect the Western Wall as a place of worship, prayer, and pilgrimage.*

# PONTIUS PILATE

**P**ontius Pilate was the Roman governor in charge of Judea, the southern portion of Israel, during the time of Jesus.

The Jewish leaders were threatened by the teachings of Jesus. They arrested Jesus and brought him to Pilate, asking that he be executed. Pilate alone had the power to condemn Jesus to death. After questioning Jesus at his trial, that is exactly what Pilate did.

Pilate was not concerned about what Jesus taught. But he cared about keeping law and order. Pilate asked Jesus if the charges against him were true, but Jesus did not answer.

During the festival of Passover, the governor could release one prisoner. Pilate asked the angry crowd that had gathered if they wanted him to release Jesus or a well-known criminal named Barabbas. They chose Barabbas.

Pilate asked the crowd what he should do with Jesus. They responded, "Crucify him!" Pilate did not think that Jesus was guilty. He could have released him, but he feared the angry crowds. He freed Barabbas and turned Jesus over to the soldiers to prepare him for crucifixion.

## KEY WORD(S)

*Crucify* comes from the word, crux, meaning "cross." Crucifixion was punishment used to put people to death, most often criminals. This gruesome form of punishment was abolished in the 4th century AD after the Emperor Constantine converted to Christianity. After that, it was claimed as a symbol of the Christian faith, no longer an instrument of death but a sign of Jesus' sacrifice and resurrection.

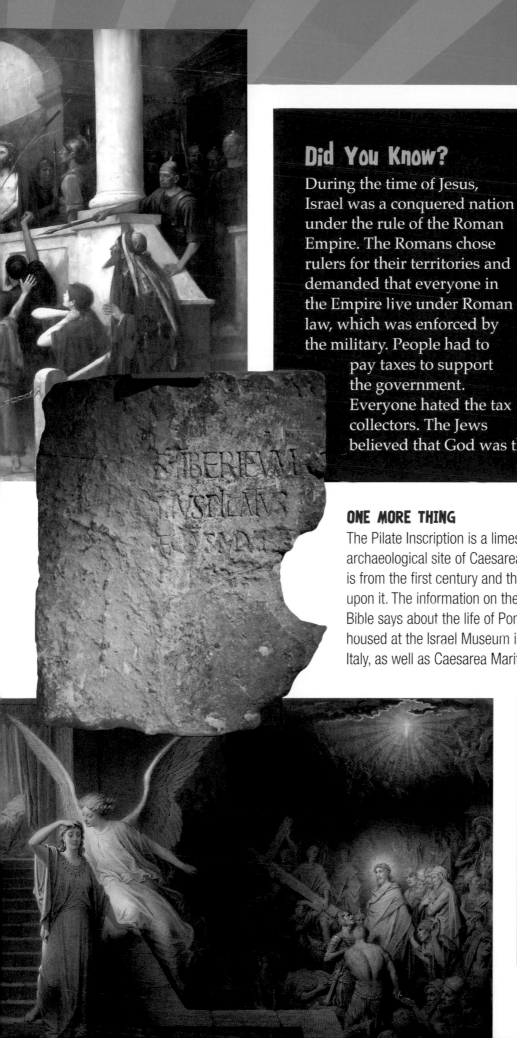

## Did You Know?

During the time of Jesus, Israel was a conquered nation under the rule of the Roman Empire. The Romans chose rulers for their territories and demanded that everyone in the Empire live under Roman law, which was enforced by the military. People had to pay taxes to support the government. Everyone hated the tax collectors. The Jews believed that God was their ruler, not the Romans.

### ONE MORE THING

The Pilate Inscription is a limestone carving found at the archaeological site of Caesarea Maritima in Israel in 1961. The stone is from the first century and the name, "Pontius Pilate," is carved upon it. The information on the stone confirms some of what the Bible says about the life of Pontius Pilate. The Pilate Inscription is now housed at the Israel Museum in Jerusalem but copies are in Milan, Italy, as well as Caesarea Maritima.

### GET A CLUE!

Who warned Pilate not to harm Jesus because he was an innocent man?

– Read: Matthew 27:19 –
While Pilate was sitting on the judge's seat, his wife sent him this message: "Don't have anything to do with that innocent man, for I have suffered a great deal today in a dream because of him."

# JUDAS ISCARIOT

**J**esus chose two disciples with the name Judas: Judas, son of James, and Judas Iscariot. Not much is known about the first Judas. But the second will be remembered as the disciple who betrayed Jesus.

According to the gospel of John, Judas acted as the treasurer for the disciples. He kept track of the money bag that held their funds. Judas protested when Mary, the sister of Martha and Lazarus, poured expensive oil on the feet of Jesus as an act of kindness, calling it a waste of money. John's gospel tells us that Judas was a thief who really didn't care about the poor but wanted to use the money for himself.

Jesus knew that Judas would betray him, yet he was invited to share in the Last Supper. That night, Judas led the soldiers to the Garden of Gethsemane where Jesus was praying. There, Judas identified Jesus to the authorities and Jesus was arrested.

Judas received thirty pieces of silver as a payment for turning Jesus over to the authorities so that they could arrest him in secret and not in front of the crowds.

## GET A CLUE!

What signal did Judas give to indicate that Jesus was the man whom the authorities were seeking to arrest?

– Read: Mark 14:44–45 –
Now the betrayer had arranged a signal with them: "The one I kiss is the man; arrest him and lead him away under guard." Going at once to Jesus, Judas said, "Rabbi!" and kissed him. **"**

## ONE MORE THING
During the final meal Jesus shared with his disciples, known as the "Last Supper," he prepared them for his upcoming death. He told them that one of them would betray him. The apostles were sure that none of them would do that, but Jesus knew. In the book of Matthew, he names Judas, and in the book of John, he shows it is Judas by handing him a piece of bread.

## KEY WORD(S)
*Iscariot* in Hebrew means, "man of Kerioth," a village in Palestine. People were often known by the town from which they came. *Iscariot* has come to refer to a person who is a traitor.

## Did You Know?
Judas was filled with regret after he betrayed Jesus. He tried to return the silver coins he had been paid, but the chief priests would not accept it. In Judaism, a person's life belonged to God. Money taken in exchange for a life was called "blood money" and considered to be a crime.

# SAUL

Saul was a respected Jewish leader in the first century. He hated the Christians. He believed them to be a threat to the Jewish faith and did his best to persecute them.

One day as he traveled on the road to the city of Damascus in Syria, a blinding light flashed all around him. He fell to the ground as a loud voice asked him, "Saul, Saul, why do you persecute me?" (Acts 9:4) Saul asked, "Who are you, Lord?" The voice answered, "Jesus," and told Saul to go on to the city where he would learn what he should do.

Saul was now blind, so his companions led him on to Damascus. God commanded a disciple named Ananias to find Saul and tell him about Jesus. Something like scales fell from Saul's eyes. Now he could see again, and he believed in Jesus. He was baptized and spent several days with the other disciples in Damascus proclaiming that Jesus was the Son of God. He then traveled to Jerusalem to join the other disciples. The Christians there were terrified of him, but Saul eventually won their trust. Saul began using his Roman name, Paul. He became a missionary, traveling from country to country to preach the good news of Jesus.

## Did You Know?

Saul began to use his Roman name, Paul, when he began his ministry with the Gentiles. It was a name more familiar to the Gentiles. His style of work with the people was to put them at ease and be open and approachable.

## KEY WORD(S)

In Greek, the word, *persecute*, means "to chase down" or "hunt." Early Christians were persecuted for following Jesus. They were literally hunted down by people seeking to harm or kill them. Saul gained a reputation as a persecutor of Christians, which is why Ananias was terrified when God told him to seek out Saul.

▶ *Pharisees were known for adding their own rules (like tithing spices) that were not in the Bible. See Matthew 23:23.*

## ONE MORE THING

Pharisees strictly followed all the laws of the Jewish faith, with little tolerance for people who disobeyed these laws. Jesus and the Pharisees were often at odds. He preached against the narrow mind-set of the Pharisees, who added other rules to the ones that had been delivered to the Jews by God. They cared only for the outward appearance of righteousness, not for a sincere heart of worship.

Philippi was a city in eastern Macedonia. Philippi was a Roman colony and its citizens enjoyed special benefits, including the right of self-government and to dress and present themselves as Romans. When the apostle Paul traveled there, he used his Roman citizenship for protection.

▲ *The Via Egnatia was a major Roman highway. Paul traveled on this roadway.*

## ATHENS

Athens was the capital city of Attica, a Greek state. Paul traveled to Athens after his journeys north of there on the Via Egnatia. When he got to Athens, he was shocked at how many idols and temples to other gods he saw there. As a result, he preached many sermons there in the synagogue and the marketplace, teaching about Christ. His longest and most famous speech referred to in the Bible (Acts 17:16–34) took place at the Areopagus, the high court in Athens. Many have renamed this place Mars Hill, since in Greece it is named after Ares (in Roman mythology, Mars), the god of war.

▲ *Many gods from different religions were worshiped in Corinth at the time Paul visited. This is the temple of Apollo, a Greek and Roman god.*

## CRETE

Crete is the largest Greek island and one of the largest in the Mediterranean. Paul left his friend Titus there to preach to the growing Christian population.

▲ *Paul was imprisoned in Philippi after he expelled a spirit from a young slave girl. Afterward, he converted the jailer and his family to Christianity.*

◀ *Artist depiction of Athens in the first century.*

## CORINTH

Corinth is in southern Greece about 50 miles from Athens. Corinth controlled two harbors and was a major trade hub. This means that many ships from different nations traveled through it selling and transporting goods. The apostle Paul traveled to Corinth after he preached in Athens. It is where he first met his friends, Priscilla and Aquila.

# PAUL THE MISSIONARY

After Saul's conversion, Christians quickly embraced him. He gained a reputation for being a respected leader and untiring advocate of the Christian faith. He traveled constantly, preaching about Jesus far and wide.

Paul gathered new believers and established churches wherever he went. He was frequently imprisoned for his beliefs, suffering under terrible conditions, but nothing shook his faith.

Legend:
- First missionary journey (A.D. 46–48)
- Second missionary journey (A.D. 49–52)
- Third missionary journey (A.D. 53–57)
- Trip to Rome (A.D. 59–60)

Paul wrote letters to the churches he established, some of them while in prison. These letters later became books in the New Testament. The books are named after the cities or geographical regions to which Paul wrote: Romans, Corinthians, Philippians. Paul wrote two letters to Timothy, a young man he befriended. Paul's letters taught the new Christians what it meant to be a follower of Christ, answered theological questions and issues, dealt with conflicts, and encouraged them to hold fast in the face of persecution. These letters continue to guide Christians and churches today.

## KEY WORD(S)

Paul's letters in the New Testament are called *epistles*, which comes from the Greek word *epistole*, meaning "news that is sent." An epistle is a letter or message. An apostle is a "messenger who is sent."

### GET A CLUE!

How does Paul describe himself in the opening sentences of many of his letters?

– Read: Romans 1:1 –
Paul, a servant of Christ, called to be an apostle and set apart for the gospel of God.

"

## ONE MORE THING

The Acts of the Apostles is a book written by the same person who wrote the gospel of Luke. More than half of Acts tells the story of Paul and his missionary journeys. Paul's epistles, or letters, are never mentioned in Acts.

## Did You Know?

It is believed that Paul was eventually executed for his faith, although this is not recorded in the Bible but rather referenced by early church historians. Without Paul, the good news about Jesus might not have spread as far so quickly.

# PRISCILLA AND AQUILA

Everywhere Paul traveled as a missionary, he gained new followers for the Christian faith. In Corinth, Greece, he connected with a Jewish couple named Priscilla and Aquila, who had previously lived in Italy. Being devout Jews at the time, they moved to Greece when Emperor Claudius ordered all the Jews to leave Rome.

Priscilla and Aquila worked as tentmakers. This meant that they were probably crafters of leather goods. Paul worked with the couple during the week and taught them about Jesus. Every Sabbath, Paul preached to Jews and Greeks in the synagogue.

Priscilla and Aquila traveled to Syria with Paul. After returning to Greece, they welcomed a new convert into their home, Apollos. He was well educated and dedicated to preaching the good news of Jesus. However, he had never heard of Jesus' baptism, only John's. Priscilla and Aquila taught him about the baptism of Jesus so that he could include this in his preaching.

Paul referred to Priscilla and Aquila as "my co-workers in Christ Jesus" who "risked their lives for me. Not only I but all the churches of the Gentiles are grateful to them." (Romans 16:3–4)

## ONE MORE THING

Early Christians were frequently persecuted for their faith. In order to identify themselves to other followers of Jesus without being obvious, they used symbols to represent themselves. One symbol was a fish. The Greek word for fish, *ikhthus*, is spelled with five letters in the original language. Each letter stands for a Greek word that describes Jesus: Jesus, Christ, God, Son, Savior. This is a fourth-century mosaic of the Greek letters of the ikhthus.

## Did You Know?

Many early Christian missionaries had to work as tentmakers in order to make a living. Tentmakers were not necessarily people who made tents but could also be skilled artists and manual laborers. People in the same trade often lived in neighborhoods where they could work together at their craft. Jews lived separately in their own sections of town.

## GET A CLUE!

What did Paul call the early Christians and how did he tell them to greet each other?

– Read: 1 Corinthians 16:20 –
All the brothers and sisters here send you greetings. Greet one another with a holy kiss.

"

## KEY WORD(S)

Priscilla and Aquila are known as two of the earliest Christian missionaries, and the first missionary couple. The Greek word *apostello* means "to send," and is also the word from which "apostle" is derived. In Latin, *mitto* means "to send," and is the root for the word "missionary," a person who is sent to tell a specific message.

# JOHN AND HIS REVELATION

The apostle John, one of Jesus' original twelve disciples, is believed to be the author of the book of Revelation. This same John is thought by some to have written the gospel of John and the books of 1, 2, and 3 John. But not all biblical scholars think he is the same John for whom the gospel is named. If this was the same

John, he was one of two brothers, along with James, whom Jesus nicknamed the "sons of thunder." They were the sons of Zebedee, a successful fisherman from the village of Capernaum. The content in Revelation is said to have come to John in a vision. Revelation is the only book of its kind in the New Testament. It is filled with symbols and images that are often frightening and violent. In Revelation, the end of time is depicted as the kingdom of God where "(God) will wipe every tear from their eyes. There will be no more death or mourning or crying or pain, for the older order of things has passed away." (Revelation 21:3–4)

**ONE MORE THING**
In Revelation, John talks about seven churches in the ancient world: Ephesus, Smyrna, Pergamum, Thyatira, Sardis, Philadelphia, and Laodicea.

**GET A CLUE!**

What does Jesus call himself in Revelation?

– Read: Revelation 21:6 –
I am the Alpha and the Omega, the Beginning and the End.

▲ *Ephesus and the Great Theater. Church tradition indicated John died in Ephesus around AD 100.*

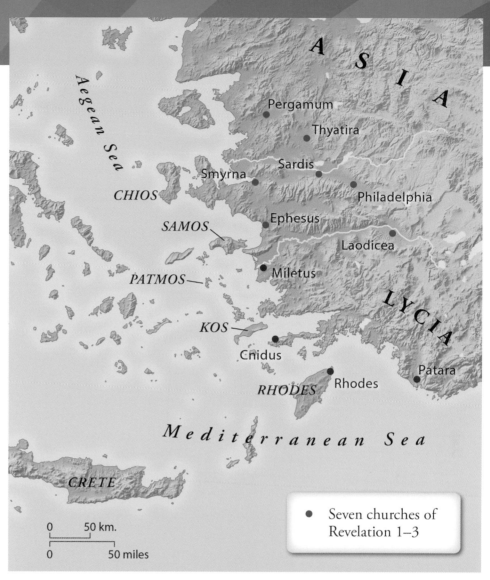

Seven churches of Revelation 1–3

## KEY WORD(S)

Revelation is also known as "The Apocalypse of John." *Apocalypse* is a Greek word that means, "disclosure," "discovery," or "revelation." The word is used in modern times to refer to the end times. Apocalyptic verses in the Bible encourage people of faith in difficult and frightening times.

# PHOTO CREDITS

Horn used for anointing   Z. Radovan/BibleLandPictures.com
Jonathan and David   © Historia/Shutterstock
Saul and the witch of Endor   Wikimedia Commons
Sword   A. D. Riddle/BiblePlaces.com, taken at the Israel Museum

### ▶ David
David as king   Wikimedia Commons
David dancing   Sweet Publishing/FreeBibleimages.org, CC BY-SA 3.0
David and Goliath   Public Domain
Helmet   A. D. Riddle/BiblePlaces.com, taken at the British Museum
Lyre   Todd Bolen/BiblePlaces.com, taken at Athens Archaeological Museum

### ▶ Solomon (and the Queen of Sheba)
King Solomon   Wikimedia Commons
Temple built by Solomon   © 2011 by Zondervan
Idol   © 2008 by Zondervan
Shalom plate   © Cherdchai Chaivimol/Shutterstock
Queen of Sheba visiting Solomon   Wikimedia Commons
Illuminated manuscript   British Library Catalogue of Illuminated Manuscripts

### ▶ Elijah and Elisha
Elijah and Elisha   Wikimedia Commons
Jewish family eating a meal   © ChameleonsEye/Shutterstock
Baal   Wikimedia Commons
Elijah being carried off in a whirlwind   Wikimedia Commons
Raven   Eric Isselee/123RF.com

### ▶ The Boy Kings: Joash and Josiah
Presentation of Joash to the people   © Historia/Shutterstock
Temple restoration   Rebuilding of the Temple by King Joash, 1602, Moller, Anton (the Elder) (c.1563-1611)/Muzeum Narodowe, Gdansk, Poland/Bridgeman Images
Scroll   Inmagine
Jehoiada teaching Joash   Review & Herald Publishing/Goodsalt
Relic of Pharaoh Necho   A. D. Riddle/BiblePlaces.com, taken at the Metropolitan Museum of Art

### ▶ Mesopotamia, Assyria, Babylon, Persia
Euphrates   © silver-john/Shutterstock
Map of the Assyrian Empire   Map by International Mapping. Copyright © by Zondervan. All rights reserved.
Map of Babylonian Empire   Map by International Mapping. Copyright © by Zondervan. All rights reserved.
Hanging Gardens   © Historia/Shutterstock
Tomb of Cyrus the Great   © Ugurhan Betin/istock.com

### ▶ Queen Esther
Esther, Haman, and king   Wikimedia Commons
Persepolis   © Wojtek Chmielewski/Shutterstock
Myrtle   Todd Bolen/BiblePlaces.com
Beauty supplies   © Sofiaworld/Shutterstock
Scroll of Esther   Z. Radovan/BibleLandPictures.com

### ▶ The Major Prophets
Isaiah   Jörg Bittner Unna/Wikimedia Commons, CC BY 3.0
Jeremiah, Ezekiel, Daniel   sedmak/123RF.com
John the Baptist baptizing Jesus   © Adam Jan Figel/Shutterstock
Scroll   © 1993 by Zondervan
Jewish captives   © 2013 by Zondervan

### ▶ Daniel
Daniel in the lions' den   Wikimedia Commons
Vegetables   serezniy/123RF.com
Writing on the wall story   Wikimedia Commons

Daniel before the king   Sweet Publishing/FreeBibleimages.org, CC BY-SA 3.0
Fiery furnace   Planet Art

### ▶ Jonah
Jonah and the fish   Wikimedia Commons
Nineveh recreation   Balage Balogh, archaeologyillustrated.com
Lots   Chris McKinney/BiblePlaces.com, taken at the Hecht Museum
Jonah sitting under a plant   Daderot/Wikimedia Commons, CC0 1.0
Jewish men praying   © Mark Lennihan/AP/Shutterstock

### ▶ The Minor Prophets
Illuminated manuscript   © Gianni Dagli Orti/Shutterstock
Widows and orphans   Library of Congress, LC-DIG-ppmsca-02746/www.LifeintheHolyLand.com
Scribe   © 1993 by Zondervan
Magi visiting Jesus   Wikimedia Commons
Temple of the Oracle of Delphi   © elgreko/Shutterstock

### ▶ The Roman Empire
Map   Map by International Mapping. Copyright © by Zondervan. All rights reserved.
Temple tax   A. D. Riddle/BiblePlaces.com, taken at the Eretz Israel Museum
Carpenter   © 2015 by Zondervan
Farmer   © 1993 by Zondervan
Roman road   Wikimedia Commons
Temple Mount   Wikimedia Commons

### ▶ Mary and Joseph
Mary and child   Planet Art
Common household in Nazareth   © 2015 by Zondervan
The Annunciation   Planet Art
Joseph as carpenter   Wikimedia Commons
Family tree of Jesus   © Historia/Shutterstock

### ▶ Jesus' First Visitors
Presentation of Jesus at the temple   Wikimedia Commons
Shepherd with flocks   Craig Dunning/BiblePlaces.com
Camel caravan   © cdrin/Shutterstock
Nativity   Wikimedia Commons
Angels appearing to shepherds   Wikimedia Commons

### ▶ Herod the Great
Herod's palace in Jerusalem   © 1995 by Phoenix Data Systems
Map   Map by International Mapping. Copyright © by Zondervan. All rights reserved.
Herod the Great   akg-images/Andrea Jemolo
Herod speaking to Magi   The Wise Men and Herod, illustration for 'The Life of Christ', c.1886-94, Tissot, James Jacques Joseph (1836-1902)/Brooklyn Museum of Art, New York, USA/Bridgeman Images
Herod's Temple   © 2016 by Zondervan

### ▶ John the Baptist
John the Baptist   Planet Art
Baptism   © Eunika Sopotnicka/Shutterstock
Anointing   © 1993 by Zondervan
Locust   © Protasov AN/Shutterstock
Honey   © DONOT6_STUDIO/Shutterstock
Salome dancing in Herod's court   Wikimedia Commons